200 CLASSIC COCKTAILS

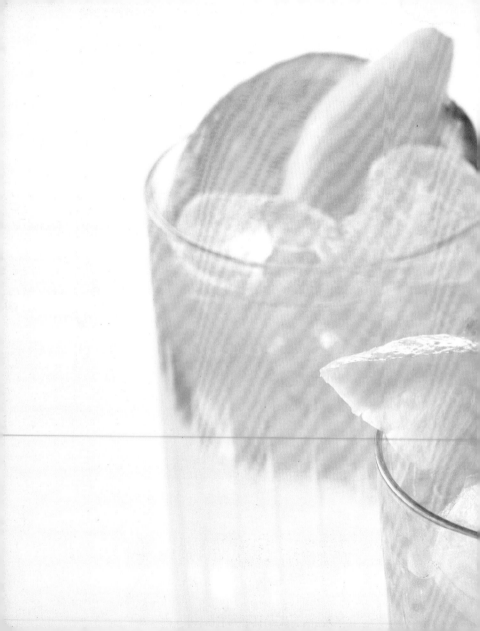

200

HAMLYN **ALL COLOUR COOKBOOK**

CLASSIC
COCKTAILS

TOM SODEN

An Hachette UK Company
www.hachette.co.uk

First published in Great Britain in 2016 by
Hamlyn, a division of Octopus Publishing Group
Carmelite House
50 Victoria Embankment
London, EC4Y 0DZ
www.octopusbooks.co.uk
Copyright © Octopus Publishing Group Ltd 2016

Tom Soden asserts the moral right to be identified as the
author of this work

ISBN 978-0-600-63132-3

A CIP catalogue record for this book is available from the
British Library

Printed and bound in China

10 9 8 7 6 5 4 3 2 1

The measure that has been used in the recipes is based
on a bar jigger, which is 25 ml (1 fl oz). If preferred, a
different volume can be used, providing the proportions are
kept constant within a drink and suitable adjustments are
made to spoon measurements, where they occur.

Standard level spoon measurements are used in all recipes.
1 tablespoon = one 15 ml spoon
1 teaspoon = one 5 ml spoon

The Department of Health advises that eggs should not be
consumed raw. This book contains some recipes made
with raw eggs. It is prudent for vulnerable people such as
pregnant and nursing mothers, invalids and the
avoid thes

This book includes recipes made with nu
derivatives. It is advisable for those with know
reactions to nuts and nut derivatives to avoid thes

It is also prudent to check the labels of pre
ingredients for the possible inclusion of nut d

The UK Health Department recommends that
women do not regularly exceed 2–3 units of
day, a unit being defined as 10 ml of pure al
equivalent of a single measure (25 ml) of spirits. T
regularly drink more than this run an increasingly
risk of illness and death from a number of con
addition, women who are pregnant or trying to
should avoid drinkin

contents

introduction   6

highballs & collins   20

fizz & froth   60

low-calorie cocktails   94

martinis & shorts   122

pressed & squeezed   172

punches & sharers   204

index   236

acknowledgements   240

introduction

what makes a good cocktail?

Good cocktails, like good food, are based around quality ingredients. Using fresh and homemade ingredients, as with cooking, can often make a huge difference between a good drink and an outstanding drink. All of this can be found in department stores, online or in kitchen shops.

cocktail ingredients

ice

This is a key part of cocktails and you'll need lots of it. Purchase it from your supermarket or freeze big tubs of water, then crack this up to use in your drinks. If you're hosting a big

party and want to serve some punches (see page 204), which will need lots of ice, it may be worthwhile finding if you have a local ice supplier that supplies catering companies, as this can be much more cost effective.

citrus juice

It's important to use fresh citrus juice in your drinks; bottled versions taste awful and will not produce good drinks. Store your fruit out of the refrigerator at room temperature. Look for a soft-skinned fruit for juicing, which you can do with a juicer or citrus press. You can keep fresh citrus juice for a couple of days in the refrigerator, sealed to prevent oxidation.

sugar syrup

You can buy sugar syrup to use when making cocktails or you can make your own. The most basic form of sugar syrup is easy to make at home by mixing caster sugar and hot water together and stirring until the sugar has dissolved. The key when preparing sugar syrups is to use a 1:1 ratio of sugar to liquid.

basic sugar syrup
makes **1 litre** (1¾ pints) of sugar syrup
dissolve 1 kg (2 lb) **caster sugar** in 1 litre
 (1¾ pints) of **hot water**.
Allow to cool. Sugar syrup will keep in a sterilized bottle stored in the refrigerator for up to 2 weeks.

You can use different types of sugar to make sugar syrup. White sugar acts as a flavour enhancer, while dark sugars have their own unique, more toffee flavours, which work well with dark spirits.

flavoured syrups

Again, you can buy these or make your own. There are three options for creating your own flavoured syrups.

The first is by adding a shop-bought flavoured essence to a sugar syrup made on a 1:1 ratio as described above. So, to make Rose Syrup, for example, add 25 ml (1 fl oz) rose essence 1 kg (2 lb) caster sugar dissolved in 1 litre (1¾ pints) of hot water.

The second technique for creating a flavoured syrup is by using fruit-flavoured tea. Make some strong fruit-flavoured tea and use this as the basis for your sugar syrup, using equal measures of tea and caster sugar. So to create 1 litre (1¾ pints) of Lemon & Ginger Syrup, for example, mix 1 litre (1¾ pints) hot lemon & ginger tea with 1 kg (2 lb) white caster sugar and stir until dissolved. Ensure that you remember to remove the tea bags prior to adding the sugar or things are likely to get very sticky!

Creating syrups from fresh fruit, herbs or spices is also very easy. The basic recipe, which you can vary, is as follows:

basic flavoured syrup

makes **1 litre** (1¾ pints) fruit syrup

250 g (8 oz) **fruit** or 3 tablespoons of **spices** (use the whole spice rather than powdered)

1 litre (1¾ pints) **water**

1 kg (2 lb) **white caster sugar**

1 Remove any thick, inedible peel from the fruit and remove any stalks, stones or pip as these will create a tannic flavour in your syrup.

2 Put the fruit or spices into a saucepan, add the water and bring the water to a rolling boil. Lower the heat and simmer for 30 minutes, topping up with water if required, or until the fruit is stripped of its colour. Taste the water to check how much of the flavour has leached into it. Spices and fruit vary in how fast they develop flavour.

3 Remove from the heat and strain into heatproof bowl. Discard the fruit or spices. Mix the hot fruit or spice liquid with the sugar until dissolved.
4 Allow to cool, decant into a sterilized bottle and store in the refrigerator until required.

to make raspberry & pineapple syrup
(see page 78), use the quantities listed below and follow the method above.

½ **large pineapple**, peeled and cubed
250 g (8 oz) **raspberries** (the riper the better and don't be afraid to use blemished fruit)
1 litre (1¾ pints) **water**
1 kg (2 lb) **white caster sugar**

to make spiced sugar syrup
(see page 216), use the quantities listed below and follow the method above.

3 **cinnamon sticks**
1 tablespoon **star anise**
2 **nutmegs**
1 teaspoon **cloves**
1 teaspoon **allspice**
1 litre (1¾ pints) **water**
1 kg (2 lb) **soft brown sugar**

ginger juice

This gives a firey, warming kick to cocktails and is very healthy. Simply run skinned ginger through a juicer or blend until smooth, then strain if no juicer is available.

cucumber juice

Incredibly refreshing, 1 cucumber will make a small glass of juice. Simply run skinned cucumber through a juicer or blend until smooth, then strain if no juicer is available.

oleo-saccharum

This is a syrup produced from the oil of citrus rind and sugar. Caster sugar dissolves best.

citrus fruit oleo-saccharum
citrus fruit
white caster sugar (allow 2 tablespoons sugar per large lemon, 3 tablespoons per orange and 4 tablespoons per grapefruit)
1 Wash the fruit. Use a vegetable peeler to peel the rind from the fruit, removing as little white pith as possible. Place the rind in a small bowl.

2 Add the sugar and press the sugar and rind firmly with a muddler, pestle or wooden spoon until the rind begins to express oils.

3 Allow the mixture to sit at room temperature for an hour until the sugar has dissolved.

shrubs

A shrub is an acidic fruit syrup that combines sugar, fruit and vinegar. Apple cider vinegars work best but you could use many different fruit and rice vinegars.

This recipe can be adapted for various shrubs.

orange & fennel seed shrub

4 oranges

1 tablespoon **fennel seeds**

250 g (8 oz) **caster sugar**

250 ml (8 fl oz) **apple cider vinegar**

1 Wash and peel the oranges. Cut the oranges into quarters. Lightly crush the fennel seeds.

2 Place the orange quarters, orange peel and crushed fennel seeds in a bowl, mix together and lightly press with a muddler, pestle or wooden spoon to release some of the juices.

3 Cover the mixture with the sugar. Mix thoroughly, cover and place in the refrigerator for 24 hours. The fruit should be surrounded by a syrup.

4 Remove from the refrigerator and lightly press again to remove any additional juices.

5 Strain the liquid into a clean bowl and scrape any remaining sugar into the bowl. Discard the fruit.

6 Add the vinegar to the liquid, then whisk until any remaining sugar is dissolved.

7 Pour into sterilized bottle and keep in the refrigerator until required.

To make camomile & fennel seed shrub (see page 42) muddle 2 tablespoons crushed fennel seeds and the zest of 1 lemon with pith removed, in the base of a glass jug to release the citrus oils. Add 250 ml each of cider vinegar and rice vinegar and 3 camomile tea bags. Infuse for 4–5 hours. Strain the liquid then add 500 g white caster sugar until dissolved. Pour into sterilized bottle and keep in the refrigerator until required.

infused spirits

Infusing your own spirits with fruit and spices is fun and easy. To infuse a spirit remove any inedible skins, stalks or pips from your chosen fruit and add the fruit to the spirit. Most fruit can sit in the spirit indefinitely but some spices need to be removed before they impart too strong a flavour. Below are recommended fruit or spice volumes along with steeping times. To infuse, place the spirit and fruit or spices in a large, sterilized sealable preserving jar and leave in a warm, dark place, such as a kitchen cupboard. The warmth will assist in the maceration. Shake the jar each day to mix the infusion.

almond-infused rum (see page 52)
Add 100 g (3½ oz) **crushed almonds** to 750 ml (1¼ pints) **rum** and leave to infuse for 3–4 weeks.

apricot-infused vodka (see page 34)
Add 250 g (8 oz) **dried apricots** to 500 ml (17 fl oz) **vodka** and leave to infuse for at least 5 days.

apricot & cinnamon-infused vodka
(see page 34)
Add 250 g (8 oz) **dried apricots** and 2 **cinnamon sticks** to 500 ml (17 fl oz) **vodka** and leave to infuse for at least 5 days.

cinnamon & nutmeg-infused bourbon
(see page 108)
Add 2 **cinnamon sticks** and 1 **whole nutmeg** to 500 ml (17 fl oz) **bourbon** and leave to infuse for 5–7 days.

cucumber-infused gin, rum or vodka
(see pages 30, 100, 206)
Add ½ medium **cucumber** to 500 ml (17 fl oz) **gin**, **white rum** or **vodka** and leave to infuse for 24 hours.

ginger-infused cognac (see page 220)
Add 200 g (7 oz) **fresh root ginger**, peeled and sliced, to 500 ml (17 fl oz) **Cognac** and leave to infuse for 2–3 days.

ginger & green cardamom-infused gin
(see page 208)
Add 100 g (3½ oz) **fresh root ginger**, peeled and sliced, and 1 teaspoon **green cardamom pods** to 500 ml (17 fl oz) and leave to infuse for 2 days.

mango-infused gin (see page 106)
Add 1 medium **mango**, peeled, stoned and chopped, to 750 ml (1¼ pints) **gin** and leave to infuse for at least 3 days.

mint-infused vodka (see page 224)
Add 5–6 sprigs of **mint** to 500 ml (17 fl oz) **vodka** and leave to infuse for 24 hours.

pineapple-infused campari (see page 112)
Add ⅓ large **pineapple**, peeled and cubed, to 750 ml (1¼ pints) **Campari** and leave to infuse for at least 3 days.

pineapple & cherry-infused rum
(see page 212)
Add ¼ large **pineapple**, peeled and cubed, 1 tablespoon **maraschino cherries** and 500 ml (17 fl oz) **white rum** and leave to infuse for at least 5 days.

raspberry-infused aperol (see page 210)
Add 250 g (8 oz) **raspberries** to 500 ml (17 fl oz) **Aperol** and leave to infuse for 7–10 days.

star anise-infused vodka (see page 150)
Add 2 tablespoons **star anise** to 500 ml (17 fl oz) **vodka** and leave to infuse for 3–5 days.

orange & cherry-infused bourbon
(see page 40)
Muddle 6 slices **orange** and 6 **glacier** cherries in a jar and add 500 ml (17 fl oz) **bourbon**. Steep for 24 hours and strain.

choosing glasses

There are thousands of different cocktails, but they all fall into one of three categories: long, short or shot. Long drinks generally have more mixer than alcohol and are often served with ice and a straw. The terms 'straight up' and 'on the rocks' are synonymous with the short drink, which tends to be more about the spirit, which is often combined with a single mixer, at most. Finally, there is the shot. These miniature cocktails are made up mainly from spirits and liqueurs and are designed to give a quick hit of alcohol. Cocktail glasses are tailored to the type of drinks they will contain.

champagne flute
Used for Champagne or Champagne cocktails, the narrow mouth of the flute helps the drink to stay fizzy.

champagne saucer
These old-fashioned glasses are not very practical for serving Champagne because the drink quickly loses its fizz.

margarita or coupette glass
When this type of glass is used for a Margarita, the rim is dipped in salt. These glasses are used for daiquiris and other fruit-based cocktails.

martini glass
A martini glass, also known as a cocktail glass, is designed so that your hand can't warm the glass, making sure that the cocktail is served completely chilled.

highball glass
A highball glass is suitable for any long cocktail, from the Cuba Libre (see page 86) to Long Island Iced Tea (see page 82).

collins glass

This is similar to a highball glass but is slightly narrower.

wine glass

Sangria (see page 206) is often served in a wine glass, but they are not usually used for cocktails.

old-fashioned glass

Also known as a rocks glass, the old-fashioned glass is great for any drink that's served on the rocks or straight up. It's also good for muddled drinks.

shot glass

Shot glasses are often found in two sizes — for a single or double measure. They are ideal for a single mouthful, which can range from a Tequila Shot to the more decadent layered B-52.

balloon glass

These glasses are usually used for fine spirits, whose aroma is as important as the taste. The glass can be warmed to encourage the release of the aroma.

hurricane glass

This type of glass is mostly found in beach bars, where it is used to serve creamy, rum-based drinks.

boston glass

Often used by bartenders for mixing cocktails, the Boston glass is also good for fruity drinks.

toddy glass

A toddy glass is generally used for a hot drink, such as Irish Coffee.

sling glass

This has a very short stemmed base and is most famously used for a Singapore Sling (see page 44).

useful equipment

There are a few tools that are worth investing in if you are planning to make cocktails.

shaker
The Boston shaker is the most simple option, but it needs to be used in conjunction with a hawthorne strainer. Alternatively you could choose a shaker with a built-in strainer.

measure or jigger
Single and double measures are available and are essential when you are mixing ingredients so that the proportions are always the same. One measure is 25 ml or 1 fl oz.

mixing glass
A mixing glass is used for those drinks that require only a gentle stirring before they are poured or strained.

hawthorne strainer
This type of strainer is often used in conjunction with a Boston shaker, but a simple tea strainer will also work well.

bar spoon
Similar to a teaspoon but with a long handle, a bar spoon is used for stirring, layering and muddling drinks.

muddling stick
Similar to a pestle, which will work just as well, a muddling stick, or muddler, is used to crush fruit or herbs in a glass or shaker for drinks like the Mojito (see page 116).

bottle opener
Choose a bottle opener with two attachments, one for metal-topped bottles and a corkscrew for wine bottles.

pourers
A pourer is inserted into the top of a spirit bottle to enable the spirit to flow in a controlled manner.

food processor
A food processor or blender is useful for making frozen cocktails and smoothies.

the spirits and their partners

Each spirit has a natural affinity with certain flavours, and it is from these complementary relationships that cocktails are born.

brandy
Much brandy is distilled from grapes, but there are some varieties that use other fruits as their base. Serve brandy with fruit and fruit juices, but don't use the finest brandies for mixed drinks.

gin
A clear grain spirit infused with juniper berries, gin was first produced in Holland over 400 years ago. Serve it with citrus fruits, fresh berries and tonic water.

rum
This Caribbean staple, which dates back to the 17th century, is made from sugar cane left over after sugar production. Serve rum with any of the exotic fruits, cream or cola.

vodka
Vodka is distilled from grain and is relatively free from natural flavour. There is fierce debate as to its origins, with both the Poles and the Russians claiming to have invented the drink. With its neutral character, it is infinitely mixable with a huge range of flavours. Serve it with cranberry, tomato or citrus juices, or for a classic drink simply add tonic water.

tequila
Mexico's best-known spirit is made from the blue agave plant, and its origins can be traced back to the Aztecs. It was traditionally served by itself as a Tequila Slammer, but also works well with citrus and sour fruits as well as ginger and tomato.

whisky
The origins of whisky are hotly debated, with both Scotland and Ireland staking a claim to having developed it from fermented grain. Modern whiskies have a much smoother taste and texture, and can be blended or unblended. Serve it with water, soda water or ginger ale.

perfecting your technique

With just a few basic techniques, your bartending skills will be complete. Follow the step-by-step instructions to hone your craft and mix perfect cocktails.

blending
Frozen cocktails and smoothies are blended with ice in a blender until they are of a smooth consistency. A frozen Daiquiri or Margarita is made using a virtually identical recipe to the unfrozen versions but with a scoop of crushed ice added to the blender before blending on high speed. Be careful not to add too much ice to the recipe as this will dilute the cocktail. It's best to add a little at a time.

shaking
The best-known cocktail technique and probably the one that you use most often, so it's important to get right. Shaking is used to mix ingredients quickly and thoroughly, and to chill the drink before serving.
1 Half-fill a cocktail shaker with ice cubes, or cracked or crushed ice.
2 If the recipe calls for a chilled glass add a few ice cubes and some cold water to the glass, swirl it around and discard.
3 Add the recipe ingredients to the shaker and shake until a frost forms on the outside. Use both hands, one at each end, so that it doesn't slip.
4 Strain the cocktail into the glass and serve.

muddling
Muddling is a technique that is used to bring out the flavours of herbs and fruit using a blunt tool called a muddler, and the best-known muddled drink is the Mojito (see page 116).
1 Add mint leaves to a highball glass. Add some sugar syrup and some lime wedges.
2 Hold the glass firmly and use a muddler or pestle to press down. Twist and press to release the flavours.
3 Continue this for about 30 seconds, then top up the glass with crushed ice and add the remaining ingredients.

building

This is a straightforward technique that involves nothing more than putting the ingredients together in the correct order.
1 Have all the ingredients for the cocktail to hand. Chill the glass, if required.
2 Add each ingredient in recipe order, making sure that all measures are exact.

double-straining

When you want to prevent all traces of puréed fruit and ice fragments from entering the glass, use a shaker with a built-in strainer in conjunction with a hawthorne strainer. Alternatively, strain through a fine strainer.

layering

A number of spirits can be served layered on top of each other, and because some spirits are lighter than others they will float on top of your cocktail. One of the best-known layered drinks is the Grasshopper (see page 162).
1 Pour the first ingredient into a glass, taking care that it does not touch the sides.
2 Position a bar spoon in the centre of the glass, rounded part down and facing you. Rest the spoon against the side of the glass as your pour the second ingredient down the spoon. It should float on top of the first liquid, creating a separate layer.
3 Repeat with the third ingredient, then carefully remove the spoon.

stirring

A cocktail is prepared by stirring when the ingredients need to be mixed and chilled but it's important to maintain the clarity. This ensures that there is no fragmented ice and no air bubbles throughout the drink. Some stirred cocktails require the ingredients to be prepared in a mixing glass, then strained into the serving glass with a fine strainer.
1 Add the ingredients to a glass in the order stated in the recipe.
2 Use a bar spoon to stir the drink, lightly or vigorously, as described in the recipe.
3 Finish the drink with any decoration and serve.

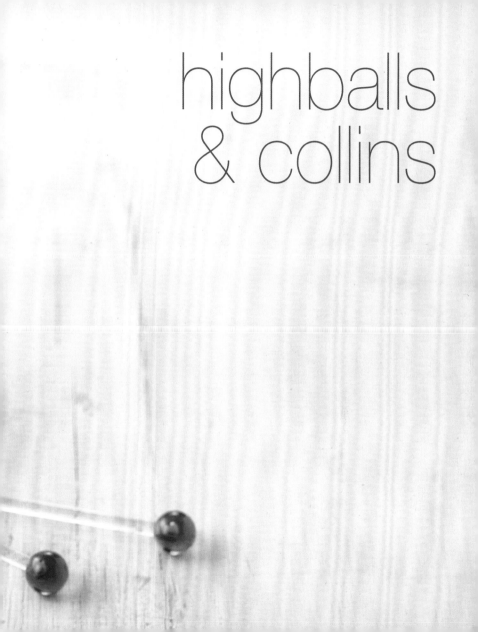

highballs
& collins

tom collins

makes **1**
glass **collins**
equipment **cocktail shaker,
 strainer**

2 measures **gin**
1 measure **sugar syrup**
1 measure **lemon juice**
ice cubes
4 measures **soda water**

To decorate
lemon wedge
black cherry

Put the gin, sugar syrup and lemon juice into a cocktail shaker and fill with ice cubes.

Shake then strain into a glass full of ice cubes and top up with the soda water. Decorate with a lemon wedge and a cherry and serve.

For a Ginty Collins, pour 2 measures gin into a collins glass and add 1 Earl Grey tea bag. Allow to steep for 1 minute before removing the tea bag. Fill the glass with ice cubes and add 1 measure lemon juice, 1 measure sugar syrup, 2 teaspoons grapefruit liqueur and 2 dashes grapefruit bitters and stir gently. Decorate with a grapefruit twist and serve.

whisky highball

makes **1**
glass **collins**

ice cubes
2 measures **Scotch whisky**
1 dash **Angostura bitters**
4 measures **soda water**
lemon twist, to decorate

Add 3 large ice cubes and the whisky and Angostura bitters to a glass. Stir gently, then fill the glass with more ice cubes and top up with the soda water. Decorate with a lemon twist and serve.

For an Ichi Highball, add 4 cucumber slices, 1 measure umeshu and 1 ½ measures Scotch whisky to a glass and press the cucumber with the end of a bar spoon to release some of the flavour. Fill a collins glass with ice cubes, then top with 4 measures soda water and stir. Decorate with a cucumber strip and serve.

berry collins

makes **2**
glasses **highball**
equipment **muddler**

8 **raspberries**, plus extra to
   decorate
8 **blueberries**, plus extra to
   decorate
1–2 dashes **strawberry syrup**
crushed ice
4 measures **gin**
4 teaspoons **lemon juice**
sugar syrup, to taste
soda water, to top up
lemon slices, to decorate

Muddle the berries and strawberry syrup in the bottom
of each glass, then fill each glass with crushed ice.

Add the gin, lemon juice and sugar syrup. Stir, then top
up with the soda water. Decorate with berries and lemon
slices and serve.

For a Lemon Grass Collins, divide 4 measures
lemon grass vodka (see infused spirits, page 12)
between 2 highball glasses full of crushed ice, then
add ½ measure vanilla liqueur and 1 dash lemon juice
to each. Add sugar syrup to taste and top up with
ginger beer.

playa del mar

makes **2**
glasses **highball**
equipment **cocktail shaker,
  strainer**

2 **orange slices**
light brown sugar and **sea
  salt**, mixed
ice cubes
2½ measures **tequila gold**
1½ measures **Grand Marnier**
4 teaspoons **lime juice**
1½ measures **cranberry juice**
1½ measures **pineapple juice**

To decorate
pineapple wedges
orange rind spirals

Frost the rim of each glass by moistening it with an orange slice, then pressing it into the sugar and salt mixture.

Fill each glass with ice cubes. Pour the tequila, Grand Marnier and fruit juices into a cocktail shaker. Fill the shaker with ice cubes and shake vigorously for 10 seconds, then strain into the glasses. Decorate each glass with a pineapple wedge and an orange rind spiral.

For a Sunburn, fill 2 highball glasses with ice, add 2 measures tequila gold, 1 tablespoon Cointreau and 6 measures cranberry juice to each. Decorate with orange slices, if you like.

gin cucumber cooler

makes **1**
glass **collins**
equipment **muddler**

2 measures **gin**
5 **mint leaves**, plus an extra
    sprig to decorate
5 slices **cucumber**
3 measures **apple juice**
3 measures **soda water**
ice cubes

Add the gin, mint and cucumber to a glass and gently muddle.

Leave to stand for a couple of minutes, then add the apple juice, soda water and some ice cubes. Decorate with a sprig of mint and serve.

For an Eden's Club Collins, add 2 measures cucumber-infused gin (see page 12), 2 teaspoons elderflower liqueur, 5 mint leaves, 2 teaspoons lemon juice and 2 measures apple juice to a cocktail shaker. Shake and strain into an ice-filled sling glass. Top up with 3 measures soda water, decorate with an apple slice or mint sprig and serve.

sea breeze

makes **2**
glasses **highball**

ice cubes
2 measures **vodka**
4 measures **cranberry juice**
2 measures **grapefruit juice**
lime wedges, to decorate

Fill 2 highball glasses with ice cubes, pour over the vodka, cranberry juice and grapefruit juice and stir well.

Decorate with lime wedges and serve.

For a Bay Breeze, replace the grapefruit juice with pineapple juice.

apricot collins

makes **1**
glass **collins**
equipment **cocktail shaker,
   strainer**

2 measures **apricot-infused
   vodka** (see page 12)
1 measure **lemon juice**
1 measure **sugar syrup**
ice cubes
4 measures **soda water**
apricot wedge, to decorate

Add the vodka, lemon juice and sugar syrup to a cocktail shaker, then fill with ice cubes.

Shake and strain into a glass filled with ice cubes. Top up with the soda water, decorate with an apricot wedge and serve.

For a Blossom Tree Fizz, add 2 measures apricot & cinnamon-infused vodka (see page 12), ½ teaspoon orange blossom water, 3 teaspoons sugar syrup, 4 teaspoons lemon juice, 1 measure orange juice and 3 teaspoons egg white to a cocktail shaker. Whisk thoroughly, then add some ice cubes. Shake hard, then add 4 measures soda water and strain into an ice-filled sling glass. Decorate with grated orange zest and serve.

tijuana mary

makes **1**
glass **collins**
equipment **cocktail shaker,
 muddler, strainer**

4 chunks **watermelon**, plus
 extra to decorate
2 measures **tequila**
2 teaspoons **sriracha sauce**
1 pinch **salt**
2 pinches **pink peppercorns**
ice cubes
4 measures **tomato juice**

Place the watermelon chunks in a cocktail shaker
and muddle. Add the tequila, sriracha sauce, salt,
peppercorns and some ice cubes and shake.

Strain into a glass full of ice cubes and top up
with the tomato juice. Stir well, decorate with
a watermelon wedge and serve.

For a Summer Mary, add 2 measures vodka,
2 teaspoons lime juice, 1 measure orange juice,
2 teaspoons sweet chilli sauce, 2 pinches celery
salt and 4 measures tomato juice to a collins glass.
Top up with ice cubes. Score a celery stick to release
its flavours, add to the glass and serve.

Monte Carlo sling

makes **2**

glasses **highball**

equipment **muddling stick,
cocktail shaker, strainer,
cocktail sticks**

10 **seedless grapes**, plus
extra to decorate

crushed **ice**

2 measures **brandy**

1 measure **peach liqueur**

2 measures **ruby port**

2 measures **lemon juice**

1 measure **orange juice**

2 dashes **orange bitters**

4 measures **Champagne**

Muddle 5 grapes in the base of each highball glass, then fill the glass with crushed ice.

Put all the other ingredients, except the Champagne, into a cocktail shaker and add more ice. Shake well and strain into the glasses. Top up with the Champagne, decorate with grapes and serve.

For a Fuzzy Navel, to serve 1, one of the easiest cocktails to prepare, simply pour 1½ measures of peach liqueur into a highball glass. Add plenty of ice and top up with fresh orange juice.

bourbon mule

makes **1**
glass **collins**

ice cubes
2 measures **bourbon**
3 teaspoons **orange liqueur**
2 teaspoons **lemon juice**
4 measures **ginger beer**
2 dashes **Angostura bitters**
lemon and **lime wedge**, to
  decorate

Fill a glass with ice cubes, add the remaining
ingredients and stir.

Decorate with a lemon and a lime wedge and serve.

For a Cherry Buck Mule, fill a collins glass with
ice cubes, add 2 measures orange & cherry-infused
bourbon (see page 13), 4 teaspoons Triple Sec, 2
teaspoons lemon juice and 2 teaspoons ginger juice
and stir. Top up with 4 measures soda water, decorate
with a maraschino cherry or orange slice and serve.

camomile collins

makes **1**
glass **collins**

2 measures **gin**
1 **camomile tea bag**
ice cubes
1 measure **lemon juice**
1 measure **sugar syrup**
4 measures **soda water**
ice cubes
lemon slice, to decorate

Pour the gin into a glass and add the tea bag. Stir the tea bag and gin together until the gin is infused with camomile flavour, about 5 minutes. Remove the tea bag and fill the glass with ice cubes

Add the remaining ingredients, decorate with a lemon slice and serve.

For an Orchard Collins, add 1 measure gin, 3 teaspoons lemon juice, 3 teaspoons camomile & fennel seed shrub (see page 11) and 1 measure apple juice to a cocktail shaker and shake. Strain into a collins glass filled with ice cubes and top up with 4 measures cider. Decorate with an apple slice and serve.

singapore sling

makes **2**
glasses **highball**
equipment **cocktail shaker,
  strainer**

ice cubes
2 measures **gin**
1 measure **cherry brandy**
½ measure **Cointreau**
½ measure **Bénédictine**
1 measure **grenadine**
1 measure **lime juice**
10 measures **pineapple juice**
1–2 dashes **Angostura bitters**

To decorate
pineapple wedges
maraschino cherries

Half-fill a cocktail shaker with ice cubes and put some ice cubes into each highball glass. Add the remaining ingredients to the shaker and shake until a frost forms on the outside of the shaker.

Strain over the ice cubes into the glasses. Decorate each one with a pineapple wedge and a maraschino cherry and serve.

For a Gin Sling, shake the juice of 1 lemon, 2 measures cherry brandy and 6 measures gin with plenty of ice. Strain into 2 highball glasses filled with ice and top up with soda water.

scotch ginger highball

makes **1**
glass **collins**

ice cubes
2 measures **Scotch whisky**
1 measure **lemon juice**
3 teaspoons **sugar syrup**
4 measures **ginger ale**
slice **fresh root ginger**, to
   decorate

Pour the whisky, lemon juice, sugar syrup and ginger ale into a glass filled with ice cubes and stir.

Decorate with a slice of fresh root ginger and serve.

For a Highland Highball, add 2 measures Scotch whisky, 3 teaspoons citrus oleo-saccharum (see page 10), 2 teaspoons ginger juice, 2 teaspoons lemon juice and 2 dashes Angostura bitters to a cocktail shaker and fill with ice. Strain into a collins glass filled with ice cubes, then top up with 4 measures soda water. Decorate with lemon wedge and crystallized ginger and serve.

los altos

makes **1**
glass **collins**
equipment **cocktail shaker,
  muddler, strainer**

5 slices **tangerine**
3 teaspoons **agave syrup**
2 measures **tequila**
2 teaspoons **lime** juice
2 teaspoons **Campari**
ice cubes
4 measures **soda water**

To decorate
orange slice
lime wedge

Add the tangerine slices and agave syrup to a cocktail shaker and muddle.

Pour in the tequila, lime juice and Campari and shake. Strain into a glass filled with cubed ice and top up with the soda water. Decorate with an orange slice and a lime wedge and serve.

For a Paloma, pour 2 measures tequila, 3 measures white grapefruit juice and 3 measures lemon or lime soda into a collins glass filled with cubed ice and stir. Decorate with a lime slice and serve.

apple jack ricky

makes **1**
glass **collins**
equipment **cocktail shaker,
  strainer**

2 measures **apple brandy**
2 measures **pink grapefruit
  juice**
2 teaspoons **sugar syrup**
ice cubes
4 measures **soda water**
pink grapefruit wedge, to
  decorate

Add apple brandy, grapefruit juice and sugar syrup to
a cocktail shaker.

Shake and strain into an ice-filled glass before topping
up with the soda water. Decorate with a pink grapefruit
wedge and serve.

For a Dusky Ricky, add 2 measures apple brandy,
4 teaspoons lemon juice, 3 teaspoons maple syrup,
1 measure orange juice and 1 measure pink grapefruit
juice to a cocktail shaker and fill with ice cubes. Shake
and strain in to an ice-filled collins glass. Top up with
2 measures soda water, decorate with a grapefruit twist
and serve.

tahitian mule

ice cubes
1 measure **amber rum**
2 teaspoons **lime juice**
3 teaspoons **orange liqueur**
3 measures **ginger beer**
lime and **orange slice**, to
    decorate

Fill a glass with ice. Pour rum, lime juice, orange liqueur and ginger beer into the glass and stir.

Decorate with lime and orange slices and serve.

For Baijan Punch, fill a cocktail shaker with ice. Add 2 measures almond-infused rum (see page 12), 2 teaspoons ginger juice, 1 measure pineapple juice, 2 teaspoons falernum, 2 teaspoons lime juice and 2 dashes Angostura bitters and shake. Strain into a sling glass filled with ice cubes and top up with 4 measures soda water. Decorate with a pineapple wedge or lime slice and serve.

mexican mule

makes **2**
glasses **highball**
equipment **muddler**

2 **limes**
2 dashes **sugar syrup**
crushed ice
2 measures **José Cuervo
  Gold tequila**
2 measures **Kahlúa coffee
  liqueur**
ginger ale, to top up

Cut the limes into wedges. Put half in each highball glass and muddle with the sugar syrup.

Half-fill each glass with crushed ice, add the tequila and Kahlúa, stir and top up with ginger ale.

For a Moscow Mule, put 6–8 cracked ice cubes in a cocktail shaker, add 4 measures vodka and the juice of 4 limes and shake well. Pour, without straining, into 2 highball glasses over ice and top up with ginger beer.

ginger fix

makes **1**
glass **collins**

ice cubes
1 measure **blended Scotch whisky**
1 measure **ginger wine**
2 dashes **Angostura bitters**
4 measures **soda water**
lemon wedge, to decorate

Fill the glass with ice cubes, add the remaining ingredients and stir.

Decorate with a lemon wedge and serve.

For a Highland Punch, add 1½ measures blended Scotch whisky, 3 teaspoons Drambuie, 1 measure lemon juice, 3 teaspoons honey, 2 teaspoons fresh ginger juice, 2 dashes Angostura bitters to a cocktail shaker. Shake, strain into a sling glass filled with ice cubes and top up with 4 measures soda water. Decorate with crystallized ginger and serve.

sex on the beach

makes **2**
glasses **highball**
equipment **cocktail shaker,
   strainer**

ice cubes
2 measures **vodka**
2 measures **peach schnapps**
2 measures **cranberry juice**
2 measures **orange juice**
2 measures **pineapple juice**
   (optional)

To decorate
lemon wedges
lime wedges

Put 8–10 ice cubes into a cocktail shaker and add the vodka, schnapps, cranberry juice, orange juice and pineapple juice (if used). Shake well.

Put 3–4 ice cubes into each highball glass, strain over the cocktail. Decorate with lemon and lime wedges and serve.

For Sex in the Dunes, replace the cranberry juice and orange juice with 1 measure Chambord, shake well and decorate each glass with pineapple chunks.

rossini

makes **1**
glass **flute**
equipment **food processor,
  strainer**

4 **strawberries**
2 teaspoons **sugar syrup**
5 measures **prosecco**, chilled

Put the strawberries and sugar syrup into a food processor or blender and blend until smooth.

Strain into a flute glass, top with the prosecco and serve.

For a Parisian Fizz, add 4 teaspoons raspberry purée, 2 teaspoons passion fruit pulp, 1 teaspoon sugar syrup, 1 teaspoon pastis and 4 measures chilled prosecco to a flute glass and stir. Decorate with a raspberry and serve.

bucks fizz

makes **1**
glass **flute**

2 measures **fresh orange juice**, chilled
1 measure **sloe gin**, chilled
2 measures **prosecco**, chilled
orange twist, to decorate

Pour all the ingredients into a flute glass, decorate with an orange twist and serve.

For a St Marks Fizz, add 1 measure Aperol, 1 measure pink grapefruit juice, 2 teaspoons passion fruit syrup and 3 measures chilled prosecco to a wine glass full of ice cubes and stir. Decorate with a grapefruit wedge and serve.

french 75

makes **1**
glass **flute**
equipment **cocktail shaker,
   strainer**

1 measure **gin**
3 teaspoons **lemon juice**
3 teaspoons **sugar syrup**
4 measures **Champagne**,
   chilled
lemon twist, to decorate

Add the gin, lemon juice and sugar syrup to a cocktail shaker and shake.

Strain into a flute glass and top up with the Champagne. Decorate with a lemon twist and serve.

For a French Afternoon, add 1 measure gin, 3 teaspoons camomile tea syrup (see page 9), 3 teaspoons lemon juice and 2 dashes peach bitters to a cocktail shaker. Shake and strain into a flute glass. Top up with 4 measures chilled Champagne, decorate with a lemon twist and serve.

valencian sangria

makes **1**
glass **wine glass**

ice cubes
1 measure **brandy**
2 measures **blood orange juice**
1 pinch **pink peppercorns**
1 measure **sweet vermouth**
2 teaspoons **Campari**
2 measures **red wine**
2 measures **soda water**
orange slice, to decorate

Fill a wine glass with ice cubes. Add all the remaining ingredients and stir.

Decorate with an orange slice and serve.

For Bitter Sweet Sangria, fill a large wine glass with ice cubes, add 1 measure orange liqueur, 1 measure sweet vermouth, 2 teaspoons Campari, 2 measures red wine, 2 measures lemonade and stir. Decorate with an orange slice and serve.

zan la cay

makes **1**
glass **flute**
equipment **cocktail shaker,
  muddler, strainer**

5 cm (2 in) piece **cucumber**
1 **green cardamom pod**
3 teaspoons **crème de peche**
2 teaspoons **sugar syrup**
ice cubes
4 measures **Champagne**,
  chilled
cucumber slice, to decorate

Muddle the cucumber and cardamom pod at the base of a cocktail shaker then add the crème de peche and sugar syrup.

Add a couple of ice cubes, pour in the Champagne and stir before straining into a flute glass.

Decorate with a cucumber slice and serve.

For a Bali Fizz, add 1 measure bison grass vodka, 3 teaspoons peach juice, 1 green cardamom pod, 1 measure cucumber juice, 2 teaspoons lemon juice and 2 teaspoons sugar syrup to a cocktail shaker. Shake, then strain into a flute glass. Top up with 3 measures chilled Champagne, decorate with a cucumber slice and serve.

ambika bellini

makes **1**
glass **flute**
equipment **food processor,**
  strainer

4 cubes **fresh mango**, about
  2 cm (¾ inch) each
1 teaspoon **grenadine**
5 measures **prosecco**, chilled

Put the mango and grenadine into a food processor or blender and blend until smooth.

Strain into a flute glass, top with the prosecco and serve.

For a Nehru, put 4 cubes fresh mango, 1 measure gin and 5 pink peppercorns into a food processor or blender and blend until smooth. Strain into a flute glass, top up with 4 measures chilled prosecco and serve.

cotter kir

makes **1**
glass **wine glass**

ice cubes
2 teaspoons **crème de cassis**
2 teaspoons **crème de framboise**
1 measure **cranberry juice**
3 measures **rosé wine**
3 measures **soda water**
raspberries, to decorate

Fill a wine glass with ice cubes. Add the remaining ingredients and stir.

Decorate with a couple of raspberries and serve.

For a Kir Royale, add 1 measure crème de cassis and 5 measures chilled prosecco to a flute glass and mix. Expel the oils from a lemon twist into the glass by twisting the rind over the cocktail, then drop the lemon twist into the glass and serve.

cobbler fizz

makes **1**
glass **flute**
equipment **cocktail shaker,
    muddler, strainer**

3 slices **mandarin**
2 **raspberries**, plus extra to
    decorate
2 teaspoons **sugar syrup**
1 measure **fino sherry**
4 measures **prosecco**, chilled

Add the mandarin, raspberries and sugar syrup to
a cocktail shaker and muddle.

Add the sherry and shake. Strain into a flute glass
and top up with the prosecco.

Decorate with a raspberry and serve.

For a Royal Cobbler, add 3 teaspoons gin,
3 teaspoons fino sherry, 3 teaspoons raspberry
& pineapple syrup (see page 10) and 2 teaspoons
lemon juice to a cocktail shaker and shake. Strain
into a flute glass. Top up with 3 measures chilled
prosecco, decorate with an orange twist and serve.

primrose fizz

makes **1**
glass **small wine glass**
equipment **muddler, strainer**

4 **mint leaves**
ice cubes
4 teaspoons **elderflower liqueur**
1 measure **apple juice**
4 measures **Champagne**, chilled
apple slice, to decorate

Bruise the mint leaves and then place them in a wine glass.

Fill the glass with ice cubes, add the remaining ingredients and stir. Decorate with an apple slice and serve.

For a Sunshine State, add 4 teaspoons gin, 3 teaspoons elderflower liqueur, 2 teaspoons lemon juice, 2 dashes peach bitters, 1 measure apple juice and 3 mint leaves to a cocktail shaker and shake. Strain into a wine glass and top with 3 measures chilled prosecco. Decorate with a strawberry and serve.

long island iced tea

makes **2**

glasses **highball**

equipment **cocktail shaker,
  strainer**

1 measure **vodka**

1 measure **gin**

1 measure **white rum**

1 measure **tequila**

1 measure **Cointreau**

1 measure **lemon juice**

ice cubes

cola, to top up

lemon slices, to decorate

Put the vodka, gin, rum, tequila, Cointreau and lemon juice in a cocktail shaker with some ice cubes and shake to mix.

Strain into 2 highball glasses filled with ice cubes and top up with cola. Decorate with lemon slices and serve.

For a Camber Sands Iced Tea, shake 4 measures lemon vodka with 200 ml (7 fl oz) of Earl Grey tea, 2 measures cranberry juice, 12 mint leaves, a dash of sugar syrup, some lemon juice and plenty of ice. Strain over ice into 2 highball glasses and decorate with lemon slices and mint leaves.

golden apricot

makes **1**
glass **collins**
equipment **food processor,
  strainer**

3 tablespoons **rum**
3 teaspoons **apricot liqueur**
4 teaspoons **lime juice**
4 teaspoons **sugar syrup**
1 **egg yolk**
ice cubes
4 measures **soda water**
dried apricot, to decorate

Put the rum, apricot liqueur, lime juice, sugar syrup and egg yolk into a food processor or blender and blend.

Strain into a glass and fill the glass with ice cubes before topping up with the soda water. Decorate with a dried apricot and serve.

For Wrong Island Spiced Tea, add 1 yellow tea bag to a cup of boiling water and leave to cool. Place 1 measure spiced rum, 2 teaspoons apricot liqueur, 1 teaspoon ginger juice, 3 teaspoons lime juice, 3 teaspoons sugar syrup and 2 dashes Angostura bitters in a soda syphon. Add 4 measures of the cooled yellow tea and charge with carbon dioxide, following the manufacturer's instructions. Chill in the refrigerator before serving in an ice sling glass, decorated with crystallized ginger.

cuba libre

makes **2**
glasses **highball**
equipment **straws**

ice cubes
4 measures **golden rum**, such
as Havana Club 3-year-old
juice of **1 lime**
cola, to top up
lime wedges

Fill 2 highball glasses with ice cubes. Pour over the rum and lime juice and stir.

Top up with cola, decorate with lime wedges and serve with straws.

For a Lucha Libre, fill a tall collins glass with cubed ice. Add 2 measures each blanco tequila, cola, soda water, ½ measure each triple sec and lime juice, and 2 dashes orange bitters. Stir to mix and garnish with 2 lime wedges.

ginny gin fizz

makes **1**
glass **wine glass**
equipment **cocktail shaker,
   strainer**

1 **camomile tea bag**
2 measures **gin**
1 measure **sugar syrup**
1 measure **lemon juice**
3 teaspoons **egg white**
ice cubes
3 measures **soda water**
lemon twist, to decorate

Place the tea bag and gin in a cocktail shaker and leave to infuse for 2 minutes. Remove the tea bag, add the sugar syrup, lemon juice and egg white. Fill the shaker with ice cubes.

Shake and strain into a wine glass filled with ice cubes and top up with the soda water.

Decorate with a lemon twist and serve.

For a Strawberry Fields, place 1 camomile tea bag and 2 measures gin in a cocktail shaker and leave to infuse for 2 minutes. Remove the tea bag, add 1 measure strawberry purée, 2 teaspoons lemon juice, 1 measure double cream and 3 teaspoons egg white to the shaker. Shake and strain into a wine glass and top up with 4 measures chilled soda water. Decorate with a strawberry and serve.

riviera fizz

makes **2**

glasses **flutes**

equipment **cocktail shaker, strainer**

3 measures **sloe gin**
1 measure **lemon juice**
1 measure **sugar syrup**
ice cubes
chilled **Champagne**, to top up
lemon twists, to decorate

Put the sloe gin, lemon juice and sugar syrup into a cocktail shaker and add some ice cubes.

Shake and strain into 2 chilled flutes. Top up with Champagne, stir, decorate each glass with a lemon twist and serve.

For a Classic Champagne Cocktail, place a sugar cube in each flute, saturate it with Angostura bitters, then add 1 measure of brandy. Top up with chilled Champagne and serve.

mandarin 75

makes **1**
glass **flute**

3 teaspoons **mandarin oleo-saccharum** (see page 10)
1 measure **orange juice**, chilled
4 measures **Champagne**, chilled
orange twist, to decorate

Add the oleo-saccharum to a flute and top with chilled Champagne.

Stir gently and decorate with an orange twist.

For a Tanka Cobbler, add 3 teaspoons mandarin oleo-saccharum (see page 10), 3 raspberries, 1 measure fino sherry, 1 measure chilled blood orange juice and 3 measures chilled Champagne to a cocktail shaker and shake. Strain into a flute glass and, decorate with a raspberry and serve.

low-calorie cocktails

rum collins

makes **1**
glass **collins**

2 measures **white rum**
1 teaspoon **caster sugar**
1 dash **orange bitters**
2 teaspoons **lemon juice**
ice cubes
3 measures **soda water**
lemon and **orange wedges**,
  to decorate

Add the rum and sugar to a glass and stir until
the sugar has dissolved. Add orange bitters and
lemon juice.

Fill the glass with ice cubes, top up with the soda
water, then stir. Decorate with a lemon and orange
wedge and serve.

For a Baijan Swizzle, add 1 measure white rum,
3 teaspoons falernum, 4 teaspoons lime juice,
5 mint leaves and 2 dashes Angostura bitters to
a sling glass half filled with crushed ice and swizzle
the drink by spinning a bar spoon between the two flat
palms of your hand. Top the glass up with crushed ice,
decorate with a mint sprig and serve.

bitter spring

makes **1**
glass **old-fashioned glass**

1 measure **Aperol**
2 measures **grapefruit juice**
4 measures **soda water**
ice cubes
grapefruit wedge, to decorate

Add the Aperol, grapefruit juice and soda water to wine glass full of ice cubes.

Stir, decorate with a grapefruit wedge and serve.

For a Venetian Sling, add 1 measure Aperol, 3 teaspoons orange & fennel seed shrub (see page 11), 2 teaspoons lemon juice, 1 measure fresh orange juice, 3 measures white wine and 2 measures soda water to a wine glass full of ice cubes and stir. Decorate with an orange slice and serve.

cucumber rangoon

makes **1**
glass **wine glass**

ice cubes
2 measures **Pimm's No. 1**
2 measures **cucumber juice**
2 teaspoons **ginger juice**
3 measures **soda water**
cucumber slice, to decorate

Fill a glass with ice cubes, add the remaining ingredients and stir.

Decorate with a cucumber slice and serve.

For a Rum Rangoon, add 1 measure cucumber-infused white rum (see page 12), 1 measure umeshu, 2 dashes Angostura bitters, 2 measures apple juice and 4 measures soda water to a sling glass full of ice and stir. Decorate with a cucumber slice and serve.

watermelon smash

makes **1**
glass **old-fashioned**
equipment **food processor**

1 measure **tequila**
4 chunks **watermelon**
5 **mint leaves**, plus an extra
  sprig, to decorate
1 teaspoon **agave syrup**
1 cup **ice**, crushed

Add all the ingredients to a food processor or blender and blend until smooth.

Pour into a glass, decorate with a mint sprig and serve.

For a Watermelon Sangrita, add 1 measure tequila, 5 chunks watermelon, 3 dashes Tabasco, 1 sprig coriander and 2 skinned green tomatoes to a food processor or blender and blend until smooth. Pour into an old-fashioned glass full of ice cubes. Decorate with a watermelon wedge and serve.

fino highball

makes **1**

glass **sling**

equipment **cocktail shaker, muddler, strainer**

4 slices **clementine**

2 slices **lemon**

1 measure **gin**

1 measure **fino sherry**

2 teaspoons **passion fruit syrup**

ice cubes

2 measures **low-calorie tonic water**

crushed ice

lemon wedge, to decorate

Muddle the fruit in a cocktail shaker, add the gin, sherry and passion fruit syrup. Fill cocktail shaker with ice cubes. Shake, then strain into a glass. Add the tonic water and fill the glass with crushed ice. Decorate with a lemon wedge and serve.

For a Citrus Highball, place 1 measure gin and 1 citrus tea bag in a collins glass and leave to infuse for 2 minutes. Remove the tea bag, fill the glass with ice cubes and top up with 4 measures low-calorie tonic water. Stir, then decorate with a lime or orange wedge and serve.

mango ricky

makes **1**
glass **collins**

5 **basil leaves**, plus extra
   leaves, to decorate
2 **lime wedges**
1 measure **mango-infused
   gin** (see page 13)
2 teaspoons **sugar syrup**
2 measures **soda water**
crushed ice

Roughly tear the basil leaves and add to a glass.

Squeeze the lime wedges over the glass and then
add them to the glass. Add the gin, sugar syrup and
soda water, then top up the glass with crushed ice.

Decorate with basil leaves and serve.

For a Peppermint Ricky, put 1 measure vodka and
1 peppermint tea bag in a collins glass and leave to
infuse for 3 minutes. Remove the tea bag and add
ice cubes to fill the glass. Add 3 lime wedges and
4 measures soda water and stir. Decorate with an
extra wedge of lime and serve.

spiced berry julep

makes **1**
glass **collins**
equipment **muddler**

1 tablespoon **frozen mixed
berries**, plus extra to
decorate
1 measure **cinnamon &
nutmeg-infused bourbon**
(see page 12)
6 **mint leaves**, plus an extra
sprig, to decorate
2 teaspoons **sugar syrup**
crushed ice

Put the berries, bourbon and mint in a glass and
muddle.

Leave to stand for 5 minutes, then add the sugar syrup
and half fill the glass with crushed ice and churn with
the muddler.

When it is thoroughly mixed, top the glass up with
crushed ice. Decorate with frozen berries and serve.

For a Mint Julep, put 1 measure bourbon and 6 mint
leaves in a collins glass and leave to infuse for 10
minutes. Add 2 teaspoons sugar syrup and half fill glass
with crushed ice before churning with a muddler. When
it is thoroughly mixed, heap the glass with crushed ice.
Decorate with a mint sprig and serve.

long blush

makes **1**
glass **sling**
equipment **cocktail shaker,
    strainer**

1 measure **vodka**
2 teaspoons **honey**
1 measure **pomegranate juice**
2 teaspoons **lime juice**
1 measure **rosé wine**
5 **mint leaves**
2 measures **soda water**
crushed ice
mint sprig and **pomegranate
    seeds**, to decorate

Add the vodka, honey, pomegranate and lime juices, wine and mint leaves to a cocktail shaker and shake.

Strain into glass and add the soda water. Top up the glass with crushed ice, decorate with a mint sprig and some pomegranate seeds and serve.

For a Passion Fruit Spritz, add 4 measures white wine, 2 teaspoons honey syrup, the pulp of 1 passion fruit and 3 measures soda water to a wine glass full of ice cubes and stir. Decorate with a passion fruit wedge and serve.

spagliagto

makes **1**
glass **old-fashioned**

ice cubes
1 measure **Campari**
1 measure **sweet vermouth**
2 measures **prosecco**, chilled
orange slice, to decorate

Fill a glass with ice cubes. Add the Campari, sweet vermouth and prosecco and stir.

Decorate with an orange slice and serve.

For an Italian New Wave, infuse 1 teaspoon of black peppercorns in 1 measure sweet vermouth for 30 minutes, then remove the peppercorns. Add the infused sweet vermouth, 1 measure pineapple-infused Campari (see page 13) and 2 measures prosecco to an old-fashioned glass full of ice cubes and stir. Decorate with a pineapple wedge and serve.

pisco collins

makes **1**
glass **collins**

ice cubes
1 measure **pisco**
2 teaspoons **sugar syrup**
2 teaspoons **lemon juice**
4 measures **soda water**
2 dashes **peach bitters**
lemon wedge, to decorate

Fill a glass with ice cubes. Add the remaining ingredients and stir.

Decorate with a lemon wedge and serve.

For a Mocking Bird, place 2 kumquats, cut into quarters, 2 teaspoons elderflower cordial and 2 teaspoons sugar syrup in a cocktail shaker and muddle. Add 1 measure grappa and 4 teaspoons lemon juice, fill the shaker with ice cubes and shake. Strain into a collins glass filled with ice cubes and top up with 4 measures soda water. Decorate with a whole kumquat and serve.

mojito

makes **2**
glasses **highball**
equipment **muddler**

16 **mint leaves**, plus sprigs to
   decorate
1 **lime**, cut into wedges
4 teaspoons **cane sugar**
crushed ice
5 measures **white rum**
soda water, to top up

Muddle the mint leaves, lime and sugar in the bottom of 2 highball glasses and fill with crushed ice.

Add the rum, stir and top up with soda water. Decorate with mint sprigs and serve.

For a Limon Mojito, muddle the quarters of 2 limes with 4 teaspoons soft brown sugar and 16 mint leaves in the bottom of 2 highball glasses, then add 4 measures Limon Bacardi. Stir and top up with soda water, if you like. Decorate with lemon and lime slices and drink through straws.

dirty sanchez

makes **2**
glasses **martini**
equipment **mixing glass,
   strainer**

ice cubes
4 teaspoons **Noilly Prat**
4 measures **gold tequila**
4 teaspoons **brine from a jar
   of black olives**
4 **black olives**, to decorate

Fill a mixing glass with ice cubes and add the Noilly Prat. Stir to coat the ice thoroughly, then pour away the excess vermouth.

Add the tequila and brine and stir until thoroughly chilled. Strain into 2 chilled martini glasses, decorate with black olives and serve.

For a Pancho Villa, shake 2 measures tequila with 1 measure Tia Maria, 2 teaspoons Cointreau and lots of ice, then strain into chilled martini glasses.

pink sangria

makes **1**
glass **wine glass**

3 measures **rosé wine**
2 teaspoons **agave syrup**
ice cubes
2 measures **pomegranate juice**
2 measures **lemon verbena tea**
2 measures **soda water**
pink grapefruit slice, to decorate

Pour the rosé wine into a glass, add 1 teaspoon of the agave syrup and stir until it dissolves.

Fill the glass up with ice cubes and add the remaining agave syrup, the pomegranate juice, lemon verbena tea and soda water.

Decorate with a slice of pink grapefruit and serve.

For Poppin's Gin Fizz, to serve 4, add 1½ measures agave syrup and 4 measures gin to a large jug and stir until the agave syrup dissolves. Fill the jug with ice cubes and add 250 ml (8 fl oz) hibiscus tea, 4 measures pink grapefruit juice and 250 ml (8 fl oz) sparkling wine and stir. Decorate with raspberries and serve.

martinis & shorts

whisky sour

makes **1**

glass **old-fashioned**

equipment **cocktail shaker, strainer**

ice cubes

2 measures **Scotch whisky**

1 measure **lemon juice**

1 measure **sugar syrup**

lemon wedge and **lemon rind spirals**, to decorate

Fill a cocktail shaker with ice cubes. Add the remaining ingredients and shake.

Strain into a glass filled with ice cubes, decorate with a lemon wedge and a lemon rind spiral and serve.

For a Penicillin, add 2 measures any Scotch whisky, 2 teaspoons Islay whisky, 2 teaspoons ginger juice, 1 measure sugar syrup and 1 measure lemon juice to a cocktail shaker full of ice cubes. Shake and strain into an old-fashioned glass filled with ice cubes. Decorate with a lemon wedge and serve.

southside

makes **1**
glass **martini**
equipment **cocktail shaker,
  strainer**

ice cubes
2 measures **gin**
4 teaspoons **lime juice**
4 teaspoons **sugar syrup**
5 **mint leaves**, plus extra, to
  decorate

Add all the ingredients to a cocktail shaker.

Shake and strain into a glass. Decorate with a mint leaf and serve.

For a Southside Royale, add 2 measures gin, 4 slices cucumber, 4 mint leaves, 3 teaspoons lime juice, 3 teaspoons sugar syrup and ice cubes to a cocktail shaker. Shake and strain into a martini glass. Top up with 1 measure chilled prosecco, decorate with mint leaf and serve.

jack rose

makes **1**
glass **martini**
equipment **cocktail shaker, strainer**

ice cubes
2 measures **apple brandy**
3 teaspoons **grenadine**
4 teaspoons **lemon juice**

Add all the ingredients to a cocktail shaker.

Shake, strain into a glass and serve.

For a Stone Jack Sour, add 2 measures apple brandy, 1 measure Triple Sec, 1 measure blood orange juice, 2 dashes orange bitters and 2 teaspoons lemon juice to a cocktail shaker filled with ice cubes. Shake and strain into an old-fashioned glass filled with ice cubes. Decorate with an orange wedge and serve.

daiquiri

makes **1**
glass **martini**
equipment **cocktail shaker,
  strainer**

ice cubes
2 measures **light rum**
1 measure **sugar syrup**
1 measure **lime juice**
lime wedge, to decorate

Add all the ingredients to a cocktail shaker.

Shake and strain into a glass. Decorate with a lime wedge and serve.

For a Baijan Daiquiri, add ice cubes, 2 measures amber rum, 2 teaspoons Campari, 4 teaspoons lime juice, 3 teaspoons sugar syrup and 1 measure pineapple juice to a cocktail shaker. Shake and strain into a martini glass. Decorate with a lime wedge and serve.

strawberry daiquiri

makes **1**
glass **martini**
equipment **muddler, cocktail
  shaker, strainer**

3 **strawberries**, hulled
dash of **strawberry syrup**
6 **mint leaves**, plus a sprig to
  decorate
2 measures **golden rum**
2 measures **lime juice**
ice cubes
strawberry slice, to decorate

Muddle the strawberries, syrup and mint leaves in the bottom of a cocktail shaker.

Add the rum and lime juice, shake with ice and double-strain into a chilled martini glass. Decorate with a strawberry slice and a sprig of mint.

For a Melon Daiquiri, shake 2 measures rum, 1 measure lime juice and ½ measure Midori with plenty of crushed ice, then strain into a chilled martini glass. Decorate with a small wedge of melon.

old-fashioned

makes **1**
glass **old-fashioned**

ice cubes
2 measures **bourbon**
1 teaspoon **sugar syrup**
1 dash **orange bitters**
1 dash **Angostura bitters**
orange twist, to decorate

Half-fill a glass with ice cubes. Add the remaining ingredients to the glass and stir for 1 minute.

Fill the glass with more ice cubes. Decorate with an orange twist and serve.

For an Old-Fashioned at Dusk, add 2 measures tequila, 2 teaspoons Islay whisky, 1 teaspoon agave syrup and 2 dashes Angostura bitters to an old-fashioned glass full of ice cubes and stir. Decorate with an orange twist and serve.

rum old-fashioned

makes **2**
glasses **old-fashioned**

6 **ice cubes**
2 dashes **Angostura bitters**
2 dashes **lime bitters**
2 teaspoons **caster sugar**
1 measure **water**
4 measures **white rum**
1 measure **dark rum**
lime rind twists, to decorate

Stir 1 ice cube with a dash of both bitters, 1 teaspoon sugar and half the water in each old-fashioned glass until the sugar has dissolved.

Add the white rum, stir and add the remaining ice cubes. Add the dark rum and stir again. Decorate each glass with a lime rind twist and serve.

For a Rum Refashioned, put a brown sugar cube in each old-fashioned glass, splash it with some Angostura bitters, then add 2 ice cubes and 2 measures aged rum to each glass, stir well then add sugar syrup to taste.

french pink lady

makes **1**
glass **martini**
equipment **cocktail shaker,**
  muddler, strainer

2 measures **gin**
4 **raspberries**
1 measure **Triple Sec**
3 teaspoons **lime juice**
1 teaspoon **pastis**
ice cubes
lime wedge, to decorate

Add the gin, raspberries, Triple Sec, lime juice and pastis to a cocktail shaker and muddle.

Fill the shaker with ice and shake, then strain into a glass. Decorate with a lime wedge and serve.

For a Margarita, add 2 measures tequila, 1 measure Triple Sec and 3 teaspoons lime juice to a cocktail shaker. Fill the shaker with ice cubes and shake. Strain into a martini glass. Decorate with a lime wedge and serve.

classic martini

makes **2**
glasses **martini**
equipment **mixing glass,
    strainer**

ice cubes
1 measure **dry vermouth**
6 measures **gin**
stuffed green olives, to
    decorate

Put 10–12 ice cubes into a mixing glass.

Pour over the vermouth and gin and stir (never shake) vigorously and evenly without splashing. Strain into 2 chilled martini glasses, decorate each with a green olive and serve.

For a Smoky Martini, put some ice cubes into a mixing glass, add ½ measure dry vermouth and stir until the ice cubes are well coated. Pour in 4 measures gin and 2 measures sloe gin then add 10 drops orange bitters. Stir well, then strain into 2 chilled cocktail glasses and add an orange twist to each.

negroni

makes **1**
glass **old-fashioned**

ice cubes
1 measure **gin**
1 measure **sweet vermouth**
1 measure **Campari**
orange wedge, to decorate

Fill a glass with ice cubes and add the remaining ingredients to a glass and stir.

Decorate with an orange wedge and serve.

For a Primera, fill an old-fashioned glass with ice cubes. Add 1 ½ measures tequila, 4 teaspoons Aperol, 2 teaspoons sweet vermouth, 3 teaspoons dry vermouth and 2 dashes orange bitters. Stir and serve.

martinez

makes **1**
glass **martini**

ice cubes
2 measures **gin**
3 teaspoons **sweet vermouth**
2 teaspoons **orange liqueur**
2 dashes **Angostura bitters**
orange twist, to decorate

Fill a glass with ice and add the remaining ingredients.

Stir, decorate with an orange twist and serve.

For a Dutch Rose, add 1 ½ measures vodka, 2 teaspoons orange liqueur, 2 teaspoons dry vermouth, 2 dashes orange bitters, 1 dash orange blossom water and 1 teaspoon grenadine to a martini glass filled with ice cubes and stir. Decorate with an orange twist and serve.

lychee martini

makes **1**

glass **martini**

equipment **cocktail shaker, muddler, strainer**

ice cubes

2 measures **vodka**

3 **lychees**, plus extra, to decorate

1 measure **Triple Sec**

3 teaspoons **lemon juice**

Add all the ingredients to a cocktail shaker and muddle.

Shake, then strain into a glass. Decorate with a lychee and serve.

For an Annabella, add ice cubes, 2 measures vodka, ½ plum, 2 lychees, 4 teaspoons rose syrup (see page 9) and 4 teaspoons lemon juice to a cocktail shaker and muddle. Shake, then strain into a martini glass. Decorate with a lychee and serve.

jaffa

makes **2**
glasses **martini**
equipment **cocktail shaker,
strainer**

ice cubes
2 measures **brandy**
2 measures **dark crème de
cacao**
2 measures **single cream**
1 measure **Mandarine
Napoléon**
4 dashes **orange bitters**
**orange-flavoured chocolate
shavings,** to decorate

Half-fill a cocktail shaker with ice cubes. Add the
remaining ingredients and shake until a frost forms
on the outside of the shaker.

Strain into 2 chilled martini glasses, decorate with
orange-flavoured chocolate shavings and serve.

For a Brandy Alexander, shake together 2 measures
each of brandy, dark crème de cacao and single cream.
Strain into chilled martini glasses and decorate with
some crumbled chocolate flake.

cosmopolitan

makes **1**
glass **martini**
equipment **cocktail shaker,
strainer**

ice cubes
1½ measures **lemon vodka**
4 teaspoons **Triple Sec**
3 teaspoons **lime juice**
1 measure **cranberry juice**
lime wedge, to decorate

Add all the ingredients to a cocktail shaker.

Shake and strain into a glass. Decorate with a lime wedge and serve.

For a Williamsburg, add ice cubes, 1½ measures star anise-infused vodka (see page 13), 2 teaspoons crème de framboise, 2 teaspoons Triple Sec, 3 teaspoons lime juice and 1 measure cranberry juice to a cocktail shaker and shake. Strain into a martini glass, decorate with a raspberry and serve.

pisco punch

makes **1**
glass **wine glass**
equipment **cocktail shaker,
muddler, strainer**

2 measures **pisco**
2 **pineapple chunks**
1 measure **orange juice**
4 teaspoons **lime juice**
2 teaspoons **falernum**
2 teaspoons **sugar syrup**
2 dashes **Angostura bitters**
ice cubes
pineapple wedge and **leaf**, to
decorate

Add all the ingredients to a cocktail shaker and muddle.

Shake, then strain into a glass filled with ice cubes.
Decorate with a pineapple wedge and serve.

For a Pisco Sour, add 2 measures pisco, 1 measure
lime juice, 1 measure sugar syrup, 3 teaspoons egg
white and 3 dashes Angostura Bitters to a cocktail
shaker. Shake, then strain into a wine glass filled with
ice cubes and serve.

abc cocktail

makes **1**
glass **martini**
equipment **cocktail shaker,
strainer**

ice cubes
1 measure **VSOP Cognac**
1 measure **tawny port**
2 teaspoons **maraschino
liqueur**
6 **mint leaves**, plus extra, to
decorate

Add all the ingredients to a cocktail shaker.

Shake and strain into a glass. Decorate with a mint leaf and serve.

For a Port Stinger, add ice cubes, 2 measures tawny port, 2 teaspoons crème de framboise, 2 teaspoons crème de cassis, 3 raspberries and 4 mint leaves to a cocktail shaker. Shake and strain into a martini glass. Decorate with a mint leaf and serve.

godmother

makes **2**
glasses **old-fashioned**

cracked **ice cubes**
3 measures **vodka**
1 measure **Amaretto di
Saronno**

Put 4–6 cracked ice cubes into 2 old-fashioned glasses.

Add the vodka and Amaretto, stir lightly to mix and serve.

For a St Petersburg, replace the Amaretto with the same amount of Chartreuse.

sombrero

makes **2**

glasses **martini**

equipment **cocktail shaker,
strainer**

drinking chocolate powder

1½ measures **tequila**

1½ measures **white crème
de cacao**

175 ml (6 fl oz) **single cream**

ice cubes

Dampen the rim of 2 chilled martini glasses and dip them into the drinking chocolate powder.

Pour the tequila, crème de cacao, cream and grenadine into a cocktail shaker and add 8–10 ice cubes. Shake vigorously for 10 seconds, then strain into the chilled martini glasses.

For a Silk Stocking, make a Sombrero, adding 4 teaspoons grenadine to the cocktail shaker. Decorate with some grated nutmeg before serving.

rising sun

makes **2**
glasses **old-fashioned**
equipment **cocktail shaker,
strainer**

ice cubes
4 measures **vodka**
4 teaspoons **passion fruit
syrup**
6 measures **grapefruit juice**
pink grapefruit slices, to
decorate

Half-fill a cocktail shaker with ice cubes and put 6–8 ice cubes into each old-fashioned glass.

Add all the remaining ingredients to the shaker and shake until a frost forms on the outside of the shaker. Strain over the ice in the glasses, decorate each with a pink grapefruit slice and serve.

For a Harvey Wallbanger, float 1 teaspoon Galliano over a mixture of 1 measure vodka and 3 measures orange juice and plenty of ice.

grasshopper

makes **2**
glasses **martini**
equipment **bar spoon**

2 measures **crème de cacao**
2 measures **crème de menthe**
mint sprigs, to decorate

Pour the crème de cacao into 2 martini glasses.

Using the back of a bar spoon, float the crème de menthe over the crème de cacao to create a separate layer. Decorate with mint sprigs and serve.

For a Banshee, shake together 2 measures crème de cacao with 2 measures crème de banane, 2 measures single cream and plenty of crushed ice, then strain into 2 chilled martini glasses.

valentine martini

makes **2**
glasses **martini**
equipment **cocktail shaker, strainer**

ice cubes
4 measures **raspberry vodka**
12 **raspberries**, plus extra to decorate
1 measure **lime juice**
2 dashes **sugar syrup**
lime rind spirals, to decorate

Half-fill a cocktail shaker with ice cubes. Add all the remaining ingredients and shake until a frost forms on the outside of the shaker. Double-strain into 2 chilled martini glasses.

Decorate with raspberries and lime rind spirals on cocktail sticks and serve.

For Watermelon Martinis, add the juice of ½ lime, 8 chunks watermelon, 3 measures vodka, 1 measure passion fruit liqueur and 1 dash cranberry juice to a cocktail shaker. Add ice cubes and shake. Strain into 2 chilled martini glasses and decorate each glass with a watermelon wedge.

gin garden martini

makes **2**

glasses **martini**

equipment **muddler, cocktail shaker, strainer**

½ **cucumber**, peeled and chopped, plus extra slices to decorate

1 measure **elderflower cordial**

4 measures **gin**

2 measures **pressed apple juice**

ice cubes

Muddle the cucumber in the bottom of a cocktail shaker with the elderflower cordial.

Add the gin, apple juice and some ice cubes. Shake and double-strain into 2 chilled martini glasses, decorate with peeled cucumber slices and serve.

For Apple Martinis, mix 4 measures vodka, 2 measures apple schnapps and 2 tablespoons apple purée in a cocktail shaker with plenty of ice cubes. Add a generous dash of lime juice and a pinch of ground cinnamon, shake and strain into 2 chilled martini glasses decorated with red apple wedges.

moon river

makes **2**
glasses **martini**
equipment **cocktail shaker,
  strainer**

ice cubes
1 measure **dry gin**
1 measure **apricot brandy**
1 measure **Cointreau**
½ measure **Galliano**
½ measure **lemon juice**
maraschino cherries, to
  decorate

Put some ice cubes into a cocktail shaker. Pour the gin, apricot brandy, Cointreau, Galliano and lemon juice over the ice.

Shake, then strain into 2 large chilled martini glasses. Decorate each with a cherry.

For Maiden's Prayers, pour 4 measures gin into a cocktail shaker with some ice, add 4 measures Cointreau and 2 measures orange juice. Shake well, then strain into 2 chilled martini glasses.

blanc mont blanc

makes **1**
glass **martini**
equipment **cocktail shaker,
muddler, strainer**

5 **white grapes**, plus extra to
decorate
1 measure **vodka**
1 measure **blanc vermouth**
1 measure **lemon juice**
1 measure **sugar syrup**
ice cubes

Muddle the grapes at the base of a cocktail shaker.
Add the vodka, blanc vermouth, lemon juice and
sugar syrup.

Fill the shaker with ice cubes. Shake and strain into
a martini glass. Decorate with grapes and serve.

For a Copa Kaye, muddle 5 red grapes at base of
cocktail shaker. Add 2 measures cachaca, 1 measure
lime juice, 1 measure sugar syrup and the pulp of
½ passion fruit. Fill the shaker with ice cubes and
shake. Strain into a chilled martini glass, decorate
with red grapes and serve.

pressed & squeezed

fresh paloma

makes **1**
glass **collins**
equipment **juicer**

½ **pink grapefruit**, peeled
ice cubes
2 measures **blanco tequila**
2 measures **soda water**
1 teaspoon **agave syrup**
pink grapefruit wedge, to
    decorate

Juice the pink grapefruit and add the juice to a glass full of ice cubes.

Add the remaining ingredients to the glass, decorate with a grapefruit wedge and serve.

For a Paloma Verde, juice 5 cm (2 inch) piece cucumber, ½ pink grapefruit, 5 pineapple chunks and 1 sprig coriander. Pour the juice into a collins glass full of ice cubes and add 2 measures tequila and 2 measures soda water. Decorate with a grapefruit wedge and serve.

stone fence

makes **1**
glass **old-fashioned**
equipment **juicer**

1 **crisp apple**, plus an **apple
    slice**, to decorate
ice cubes
2 measures **rye whiskey**
1 measure **soda water**

Juice the apple and pour into a glass full of ice cubes.

Add the whiskey and soda water. Decorate with an
apple slice and serve.

For a Stone Stairs, juice ½ Granny Smith apple and
½ pear. Pour the juice into an old-fashioned glass
full of ice cubes, add 1 ½ measures Scotch whisky,
2 teaspoons Bénédictine and 1 measure soda water.
Decorate with a pear slice and serve.

pink cooler

makes **1**
glass **old-fashioned**
equipment **cocktail shaker,
  muddler, strainer**

5 chunks **watermelon**, plus
  extra, to decorate
2 measures **lemon vodka**
ice cubes
2 measures **bitter lemon**

Add the watermelon to a cocktail shaker and muddle.
Add the vodka and shake.

Strain into a glass full of ice cubes and top up with
the bitter lemon. Decorate with a chunk of watermelon
and serve.

For a Watermelon Spritz, add 4 chunks watermelon
to a cocktail shaker and muddle. Add the lemon vodka
with 1 measure apple juice, 1 sprig mint, 4 teaspoons
lemon juice and 3 teaspoons agave syrup. Shake and
strain into a sling glass full of ice cubes and top up with
2 measures soda water. Decorate with a watermelon
slice and serve.

william's pear

makes **1**
glass **old-fashioned**
equipment **cocktail shaker,
  muddler, strainer**

½ **ripe pear** cut into chunks,
  plus an extra slice, to
  decorate
3 teaspoons **redcurrant jam**
2 measures **bourbon**
4 teaspoons **lemon juice**
2 teaspoons **sugar syrup**
ice cubes

Add the pear and jam to a cocktail shaker and muddle.

Add the remaining ingredients and shake. Strain into a glass full of ice cubes, decorate with pear slices and serve.

For Spiced Pear Punch, add ½ ripe pear, cut in to chunks, and 10 redcurrants to a cocktail shaker and muddle. Add 1 ½ measures bourbon, 2 teaspoons Bénédictine, 2 teaspoons nutmeg syrup and 2 teaspoons lemon juice and shake. Strain into an old-fashioned glass full of ice cubes, decorate with pear slices and serve.

kiwi smash

makes **1**
glass **old-fashioned**
equipment **muddler**

½ **kiwi fruit**, quartered, plus
an extra slice, to decorate
4 slices **lemon**
4 teaspoons **sugar syrup**
2 measures **gin**
1 sprig **coriander**
crushed ice

Add the kiwi fruit, lemon and sugar syrup to a glass and muddle. Add the gin and coriander and half-fill the glass with crushed ice.

Churn with the muddler until thoroughly mixed. Top up with more crushed ice, decorate with a kiwi fruit slice and serve.

For a Green Bay Colada, add 2 measures gin, ½ kiwi fruit, peeled, 4 cubes, about 5 cm (2 inches) each cantaloupe melon, 1 sprig coriander, 1 teaspoon ginger juice, 2 teaspoons lemon juice, 1 measure agave syrup and 1 cup ice cubes to a food processor or blender and blend until smooth. Pour into a sling glass, decorate with a kiwi slice and serve.

sherry punch

makes **1**
glass **old-fashioned**
equipment **cocktail shaker,
  muddler, strainer**

5 **pineapple** chunks
5 **raspberries**, plus extra to
  decorate
3 **lemon slices**
2 measures **fino sherry**
2 teaspoons **sugar syrup**
crushed ice

To decorate
pineapple wedge
raspberry

Add the pineapple chunks, raspberries, lemon slices and sugar syrup to a cocktail shaker and muddle.

Add the sherry and shake. Strain into a glass full of crushed ice, decorate with a pineapple wedge and a raspberry and serve.

For a Cobbled Summer, add 6 cubes, about 1 cm (½ inch) each, pineapple to a cocktail shaker and muddle. Add 6 teaspoons fino sherry, 4 teaspoons gin, 3 teaspoons raspberry syrup, 3 teaspoons lemon juice and 2 teaspoons sugar syrup and shake. Strain into a collins glass filled with ice cubes, decorate with a raspberry and serve.

cloudy cooler

makes **1**
glass **collins**
equipment **cocktail shaker,
muddler, strainer**

5 **white grapes**, plus extra to
decorate
4 measures **white wine**
2 measures **cloudy apple
juice**
1 teaspoon **passion fruit
syrup**
2 measures **soda water**
ice cubes

Add the grapes to a cocktail shaker and muddle.

Add the wine, apple juice and passion fruit syrup to
the shaker and shake.

Strain into a glass full of ice cubes and top with the
soda water. Decorate with a few grapes and serve.

For a Camomile Sangria, add 1 camomile tea bag
and 1 measure vodka to a cocktail shaker and leave
to infuse for 3 minutes. Remove the tea bag, add
5 white grapes and muddle, Then add 2 measures
white wine, 2 teaspoons passion fruit syrup and
1 teaspoon lemon juice. Shake and strain into a sling
glass full of ice cubes, top up with 2 measures soda
water, decorate with an apple wedge and serve.

betsy

makes **2**
glass **old-fashioned**
equipment **food processor**

2 measures **gin** or **vodka**
4 teaspoons **lime juice**
1 measure **sugar syrup**
2 **strawberries**, plus extra, to
  decorate
1 sprig **coriander**
1 cup **ice cubes**

Add all the ingredients to a food processor or blender and blend until smooth.

Pour into 2 glasses, decorate each with a strawberry and serve.

For a West Side Pink Flamingo, add 100 ml (3½ fl oz) gin or vodka, 1 measure lime juice, 1 measure strawberry syrup (see page 9), 2 measures strawberry purée, 250 ml (8 fl oz) rosé wine, 2 sprigs mint and 250 ml (8 fl oz) watermelon juice to a food processor or blender and give it short blitzes to coarsely chop the mint. Pour into a shallow freezer container and freeze for 24 hours. Remove from the freezer and stir with a fork to create a granita. Spoon into 2 wine glasses, decorate with a mint sprig each and serve with spoon.

non-alcoholic jade's cooler

makes **1**
glass **old-fashioned**
equipment **juicer**

1 **apple**
5 cm (2 inch) piece **cucumber**
1 **mint sprig**
ice cubes
3 teaspoons **elderflower
  cordial**
2 measures **soda water**
apple slice or **mint sprig**, to
  decorate

Juice the apple, cucumber and mint. Pour the juice into a glass full of ice cubes, add the elderflower cordial, stir and top up with the soda water. Decorate with an apple slice or mint sprig and serve.

For an Orchard Fizz, another alcohol-free cocktail, juice 1 apple, 5 cm (2 inch) piece cucumber, 1.5 cm (½ inch) piece fresh root ginger, peeled, 2 sprigs mint and 1 stick celery. Pour the juice into a soda syphon and add 2 measures elderflower cordial and 2 measures water. Add carbon dioxide, following the manufacturer's instructions. Chill the charged vessel in the refrigerator for 1 hour, then pour the cocktail into a flute glass, decorate with a mint sprig and serve.

non-alcoholic strawberry smash

makes **1**
glass **collins**
equipment **juicer**

6 **strawberries**
1 **apple**
2 **sticks celery**
1 **sprig mint**
ice cubes
apple slices, to decorate

Juice all the ingredients and pour the juice into a glass full of ice cubes.

Decorate with a fan of apple slices and serve.

For a Strawberry Fizz, also non-alcoholic, juice 5 strawberries, 5 raspberries 1 apple, 1 stick celery and 2 sprigs mint. Pour the juice into a soda syphon and add 2 measures cranberry juice. Add carbon dioxide, following the manufacturer's instructions. Chill the charged vessel in the refrigerator for 1 hour, then pour the cocktail into a flute glass, decorate with ½ a strawberry and serve.

caprissima da uva

makes **1**
glass **old-fashioned**
equipment **muddler**

½ **lime**, plus a wheel for
   decorating
5 **red grapes**, plus extra for
   decorating
2 measures **amber rum**
2 teaspoons **sugar**
2 teaspoons **velvet falernum**
crushed ice

Muddle the lime and grapes at the base of a glass.

Add the rum, sugar and velvet falernum and half-fill
the glass with crushed ice. Churn the mixture with a
muddler until thoroughly mixed.

Top the glass up with more crushed ice, decorate with
a lime wheel and grape and serve.

For a Caprissima da Framoesa, muddle ½ lime,
5 raspberries and 1 teaspoon pastis in a collins glass.
Add 2 measures amber rum, 2 pink grapefruit slices,
2 teaspoons raspberry liqueur, 3 teaspoons sugar syrup
and half-fill the glass with crushed ice. Churn with a
muddler until thoroughly mixed. Top up the glass with
more crushed ice, decorate with a raspberry and a pink
grapefruit wedge and serve.

duke's daiquiri

makes **1**
glass **hurricane**
equipment **food processor or blender**

2 measures **white rum**
3 teaspoons **lime juice**
1 measure **sugar syrup**
tinned peach half, drained
1 measures **cloudy apple juice**
1 teaspoon **grenadine**
1 cup **ice cubes**

To decorate
lime wheel
black cherry

Add all ingredients to a food processor or blender and blend until smooth.

Pour into a glass, decorate with a lime wheel and a cherry and serve.

For a Tahitian Pearl, add 2 measures 100 per cent agave blanco tequila, 1 measure lime juice, 4 teaspoons agave syrup, 1 tinned peach half, drained, 2 measures cloudy apple juice, 2 measures pineapple juice, 1 teaspoon grenadine, 5 mint leaves and 1 cup of ice cubes to a food processor or blender and blend until smooth. Pour into a hurricane glass, decorate with a lime wheel and a basil leaf and serve.

red rum

makes **2**
glasses **martini**
equipment **cocktail shaker, muddler, strainer**

handful of **redcurrants**, plus extra to decorate
1 measure **sloe gin**
4 measures **Bacardi 8-year-old rum**
1 measure **lemon juice**
1 measure **vanilla syrup**
ice cubes

Muddle the redcurrants and sloe gin together in a cocktail shaker.

Add the rum, lemon juice, vanilla syrup and some ice cubes.

Shake and double-strain into 2 chilled martini glasses, decorate with redcurrants and serve.

For a Rude Jude, put 2 measures white rum, a generous dash each of strawberry syrup, strawberry purée and lime juice in a cocktail shaker with plenty of ice. Shake and strain into 2 chilled martini glasses.

orange blossom

makes **2**
glasses **highball**
equipment **muddler, straws**

8 **orange slices**, plus wedges to decorate
4 teaspoons **almond syrup**
crushed ice
4 measures **pink grapefruit juice**
6 dashes **Angostura bitters**

Muddle half the orange slices and almond syrup in each glass. Fill the glasses with crushed ice and pour in the gin.

Stir, top up with the grapefruit juice and bitters and decorate with orange wedges. Serve with straws.

For The Fix, mix 4 measures gin, 1 dash lime juice, 1 dash lemon juice, 1 dash pineapple juice and 1 measure Cointreau in a cocktail shaker filled with ice. Shake and strain into 2 chilled highball glasses.

peach smash

makes **2**

glasses **old-fashioned**

equipment **cocktail shaker,
muddler, strainer**

12 **mint leaves**, plus sprigs to
decorate

6 **peach slices**

6 **lemon slices**, plus extra to
decorate

4 teaspoons **caster sugar**

4 measures **bourbon**

ice cubes, plus **cracked ice**
to serve

Muddle the mint leaves, peach and lemon slices and
sugar in a cocktail shaker.

Add the bourbon and some ice cubes and shake well.
Strain over cracked ice into 2 glasses. Decorate each
with a mint sprig and a lemon slice and serve.

For a Rhett Butler, half-fill a cocktail shaker with ice
cubes, add 4 measures bourbon, 8 measures cranberry
juice, 4 tablespoons sugar syrup and 2 tablespoons lime
juice and shake well. Strain into 2 old-fashioned glasses
filled with ice.

punches & sharers

white sangria

makes **1 large jug**

ice cubes
4 measures **vodka**
6 measures **apple juice**
2 measures **lemon juice**
2 measures **elderflower
  cordial**
6 measures **white wine**
6 measures **soda water**

To decorate
apple slices
lemon slices
mint leaves

Fill a jug with ice cubes, add all the remaining ingredients and stir.

Decorate with apple and lemon slices and mint leaves and serve.

For Sakura Sangria, fill a large jug with ice cubes and add 4 measures cucumber-infused vodka (see page 12), 1½ measures elderflower cordial, 1 measure lemon juice, 1 measure umeshu, 4 measures apple juice and 200 ml (7 fl oz) sparkling wine, then stir. Decorate with apple slices and cucumber strips and serve.

langra & tonic

makes **1 large jug**

ice cubes
200 ml (7 fl oz) **gin**
4 measures **mango juice**
2 measures **lemon juice**
2 measures **sugar**
200 ml (7 fl oz) **tonic water**
lemon wheels, to decorate

Fill a jug with ice cubes, add all the remaining ingredients and stir. Decorate with lemon wheels and serve.

For Ginger Langra, add 4 measures ginger & green cardamom-infused gin (see page 13), 4 measures fino sherry, 2 measures sugar syrup, 2 measures mango juice, 2 measures lemon juice and 200 ml (7 fl oz) tonic water to a large jug full of ice cubes and stir. Decorate with lime wheels and serve.

tinto de venezia

makes **1 large jug**

ice cubes
4 measures **Aperol**
4 measures **pink grapefruit juice**
4 measures **orange juice**
200 ml (7 fl oz) **rosé wine**
4 measures **soda water**

To decorate
orange slices
grapefruit slices

Fill a jug with ice cubes. Add all the remaining ingredients and stir.

Decorate with orange and grapefruit slices and serve.

For a Vespertilio, add 4 measures raspberry-infused Aperol (see page 13), 4 measures pink grapefruit juice, 1 measure passion fruit syrup, the pulp of 2 passion fruit and 300 ml (½ pint) chilled prosecco to a large jug full of ice cubes, stir and serve.

lola's punch

makes **1 large jug**

ice cubes
4 measures **white rum**
3 measures **lemon juice**
3 measures **sugar syrup**
3 measures **apple juice**
3 measures **mango juice**
200 ml (7 fl oz) **white wine**
250 ml (8 fl oz) **soda water**

To decorate
mango slices
apple slices

Fill a jug with ice cubes, add all the remaining ingredient and stir.

Decorate with mango and apple slices and serve.

For Colonial Punch, add 200 ml (7 fl oz) pineapple & cherry-infused white rum (see page 13), 2 measures lemon juice, 2 measures sugar syrup, 4 measures pineapple juice and 250 ml (8 fl oz) sparkling wine to a large jug full of ice cubes and stir. Decorate with pineapple wedges and serve.

earl's punch

makes **1 jug**

ice cubes
4 measures **gin**
6 measures **Earl Grey tea**
6 measures pink **grapefruit juice**
6 measures **soda water**
1 measure **sugar syrup**

To decorate
pink grapefruit slices
black cherries

Fill a jug with ice cubes. Add all the remaining ingredients and stir.

Decorate with pink grapefruit slices and maraschino cherries and serve.

For Sylvestre Punch, place 4 measures gin, 1 tablespoon marmalade, 1 measure lemon juice, 4 measures orange juice, 4 measures pink grapefruit juice, 250 ml (8 fl oz) Earl Grey tea and 6 measures mineral water in a food processor to blender and blend until smooth. Place in a soda syphon and charge with carbon dioxide, following the manufacturer's instructions. Chill in the refrigerator for at least 1 hour in the soda syphon. Pour into a large serving bottle to serve.

mulled orchard

makes **1 large teapot**

1 knob **butter**
4 measures **apple juice**
1 measure **lemon juice**
1 measure **spiced sugar
 syrup** (see page 10)
4 measures **bourbon**
6 measures **cider**
cinnamon sticks, to decorate

Melt the butter a saucepan over a gentle heat.

Add the apple juice, lemon juice, spiced sugar syrup, bourbon and cider. Stir and heat until hot.

Pour carefully into a teapot and serve in heatproof glasses, decorated with cinnamon sticks.

For Southern Belle, fill a large jug with ice cubes. Add 6 measures bourbon, 2 measures lemon juice, 2 measures sugar syrup, 4 measures yellow tea, 2 measures apple juice and 200 ml (7 fl oz) cider and stir. Decorate with apple and lemon slices and serve.

pina coco

serves **2**

equipment **food processor, straws**

1 **pineapple**

4 measures **amber rum**

1 measure **Galliano**

1 measure **coconut cream**

4 measures **passion fruit juice**

1 **banana**

1 cup **ice**

Cut the top off the pineapple and use a pineapple corer to remove the flesh inside the pineapple. Set aside the hollowed-out pineapple.

Cut the pineapple flesh into chunks. Add 7 chunks of the pineapple and the remaining ingredients to a food processor or blender and blend until smooth. Pour into the hollowed-out pineapple and serve with straws.

For rum punch, fill a large jug with ice cubes. Add 200 ml (7 fl oz) spiced rum, 4 measures lime juice, 4 measures sugar syrup, 6 measures passion fruit juice, 6 measures pineapple juice and 6 measures orange juice and stir. Decorate with orange and lime slices and passion fruit halves and serve.

la rochelle punch

makes **1 large jug**

4 measures **Cognac**
50 g (2 oz) **frozen mixed
  berries**, plus extra to serve
ice cubes
4 measures **apple juice**
2 measures **lemon juice**
2 measures **sugar syrup**
300 ml (½ pint) **ginger ale**

Add the Cognac and berries to a food processor or blender and blend until smooth. Pour into a jug. Add plenty of ice cubes and the remaining ingredients to the jug and stir. Decorate with berries and serve.

For Spice Route Punch, add 200 ml (7 fl oz) ginger-infused Cognac (see page 12) and 50 g (2 oz) frozen mixed berries to a food processor or blender and blend until smooth. Pour into a jug full of ice cubes, add 1 measure cinnamon syrup, 200 ml (7 fl oz) cloudy apple juice, 2 measures lemon juice, 1 measure sugar syrup and 200 ml (7 fl oz) soda water and stir. Decorate with cinnamon sticks and apple slices and serve.

blue grass punch

makes **1 large jug**

makes **1 large jug**

4 measures **bourbon**
3 teaspoons **marmalade**
2 measures **lemon juice**
1 measure **sugar syrup**
2 measures **cranberry juice**
6 measures **soda water**
ice cubes
dried orange wheels, to
    decorate

Add the bourbon and marmalade to a jug and stir until dissolved.

Add all the remaining ingredients and fill the jug with ice cubes. Stir.

Decorate with dried orange wheels and serve.

For Baton Blanc, put 4 measures bourbon, 2 measures lemon juice, 2 measures orange juice, 2 measures sugar syrup and 2 teaspoons marmalade in a food processor or blender and blend until smooth. Pour into a large jug, add 200 ml (7 fl oz) wheat beer and top up the jug with ice cubes. Decorate with orange wheels and serve.

watermelon punch

serves 2
equipment **food processor, straws**

1 **watermelon** (around 9 kg/20 lb)
200 ml (7 fl oz) **vodka**
20 **mint leaves**
3 measures **lemon**
5 measures **sugar syrup**
1 cup **ice cubes**
lemon wheels, to decorate

Cut the top off the watermelon and use a spoon to scoop out the flesh inside. Set aside the hollowed-out watermelon.

Remove the pips from the watermelon flesh then add the flesh and the remaining ingredients to a food processor or blender and blend until smooth. Pour into the hollowed-out watermelon, decorate with lemon wheels and serve with straws

For Afternoon Watermelon, to serve 6, add 200 ml (7 fl oz) watermelon juice, 10 strawberries, hulled, and 5 mint leaves to a food processor or blender and process until smooth. Strain and then pour into a 1-litre (1¾-pint) swing-top bottle. Add 200 ml (7 fl oz) mint-infused vodka (see page 13), 1 measure elderflower cordial, 3 teaspoons lemon juice and 500 ml (17 fl oz) soda water and stir. Chill in the refrigerator for at least 2 hours before serving.

blush sangria

makes **1 large jug**

4 measures **vodka**
2 measures **crème de
  framboise**
200 ml (7 fl oz) **rosé wine**
6 measures **cranberry juice**
2 measures **lime juice**
1 measure **sugar syrup**
6 measures **soda water**
ice cubes
edible flower petals, to
  decorate

Add all ingredients to a jug, then fill the jug with
ice cubes.

Stir and decorate with edible flowers.

For Sakura Punch, fill a large jug with ice cubes.
Add 4 measures vodka, 200 ml (7 fl oz) rosé wine,
4 measures lychee juice, 4 measures pink grapefruit
juice, 1 measure rose syrup (see page 9), 1 measure
lemon juice and 6 measures soda water and stir.
Decorate with tinned lychees, lemon slices and
maraschino cherries and serve.

torino spritzer

makes **1 large jug**

ice cubes
4 measures **sweet vermouth**
4 measures **Campari**
4 measures **Triple Sec**
4 measures **lemon juice**
200 ml (7 fl oz) **lemon** or **lime soda**
200 ml (7 fl oz) **red wine**

To decorate
lemon slices
orange slices
grapefruit slices

Fill a jug with ice cubes. Add all the remaining ingredients to a jug and stir.

Decorate with lemon, orange and grapefruit slices and serve.

For Gaseosa Tinto, add 4 measures sweet vermouth, 4 measures dry vermouth, 4 measures Campari, 2 measures orange & fennel seed shrub (see page 11), 2 measures lemon juice, 4 measures red wine and 200 ml (7 fl oz) soda water to a large jug with ice cubes and stir. Decorate with an orange wheels and serve.

pimm's cocktail

makes **2**
glasses **highball**
equipment **muddler**

ice cubes
2 measures **Pimm's No. 1**
2 measures **gin**
4 measures **lemonade**
4 measures **ginger ale**

To decorate
cucumber strips
blueberries
orange slices

Fill 2 highball glasses with ice cubes. Add the remaining ingredients, one by one in order, over the ice. Decorate with cucumber strips, blueberries and orange slices and serve.

For an On the Lawn, fill 2 highball glasses with ice and fresh fruit such as strawberries and oranges. Add 2 measures Pimm's No. 1 and 2 measures gin to each one and top up with lemonade and ginger ale.

planter's punch

makes **2**
glasses **highball**
equipment **cocktail shaker,
    strainer**

4 measures **Myer's Jamaican
    Planter's Punch rum**
8 drops **Angostura bitters**
1 measure **lime juice**
4 measures **chilled water**
2 measures **sugar syrup**
ice cubes

To decorate
orange slices
lime slices

Put the rum, bitters, lime juice, water and sugar syrup in a cocktail shaker and add some ice cubes.

Shake and strain into 2 chilled glasses. Decorate with orange and lime slices and serve.

For a Tempo, put 3 cracked ice cubes into each of 2 chilled highball glasses and pour 1 measure white rum, 1 measure lime juice and ½ measure crème de cacao into each glass. Add a dash of Angostura bitters, stir and top up with lemonade. Decorate with lime slices and serve.

garden cooler

makes **1 punch bowl**, about 5 litres (10 pints)

700 ml (1¼ pints) **London dry gin**
500 ml (17 fl oz) **lemon juice**
250 ml (8 fl oz) **sugar syrup**
250 ml (8 fl oz) **elderflower cordial**
500 ml (17 fl oz) **green tea**
500 ml (17 fl oz) **mint tea**
500 ml (17 fl oz) **apple juice**
500 ml (17 fl oz) **soda water**
ice cubes
peach slices, to decorate

Add all the ingredients to a punch bowl and stir.

Decorate with peach slices and serve.

For English Garden Fizz, add 500 ml (17 fl oz) London dry gin and 1 bunch mint leaves to a large punch bowl and leave to steep for 1 hour. Remove the mint, add 250 ml (8 fl oz) Triple Sec, 250 ml (8 fl oz) lemon juice, 250 ml (8 fl oz) sugar syrup, 250 ml (8 fl oz) cucumber juice, 250 ml (8 fl oz) apple juice, 500 ml (17 fl oz) green tea, 500 ml (17 fl oz) soda water and some ice cubes to the punch bowl and stir. Decorate with cucumber slices and serve.

index

Abc Cocktail 154
Afternoon Watermelon 224
agave syrup
Fresh Paloma 174
Green Bay Colada 182
Los Altos 48
Old-Fashioned at Dusk 134
Pink Sangria 120
Poppin's Gin Fizz 120
Tahitian Pearl 196
Watermelon Smash 102
Watermelon Spritz 178
alcohol-free cocktails 190, 192
almond syrup 200
almond-infused rum 12
Amaretto di Saronno 156
Ambika Bellini 74
Angostura bitters
Baijan Punch 52
Bourbon Mule 40
Classic Champagne Cocktail 90
Cucumber Rangoon 100
the Fix 200
Ginger Fix 56
Highland Highball 46
Highland Punch 56
Martinez 144
Old-Fashioned at Dusk 134
Orange Blossom 200
Pisco Punch 152
Pisco Sour 152
Planter's Punch 232
Rum Old-Fashioned 134
Rum Refashioned 136
Singapore Sling 44
Tempo 232
Whisky Highball 24
Wrong Island Spiced Tea 84
Annabella 146
Aperol
Bitter Spring 98
Primera 142
raspberry-infused Aperol 13, 210
St Marks Fizz 66

Venetian Sling 98
Vespertilio 210
apple brandy 50, 128
apple juice
Cloudy Cooler 186
Cucumber Rangoon 100
Duke's Daiquiri 196
Eden's Club Collins 30
English Garden Fizz 234
Garden Cooler 234
Gin Cucumber Cooler 30
Gin Garden Martini 166
La Rochelle Punch 220
Lola's Punch 212
Mulled Orchard 216
Orchard Collins 42
Primrose Fizz 80
Sakura Sangria 206
Southern Belle 216
Spice Route Punch 220
Sunshine State 80
Tahitian Pearl 196
Watermelon Spritz 178
White Sangria 206
apple schnapps 166
apples
Non-Alcoholic Jade's Cooler 190
Orchard Fizz 190
Stone Fence 176
Stone Stairs 176
Strawberry Fizz 192
Strawberry Smash 192
apricot brandy 168
apricot liqueur 84
apricots
apricot-infused vodka 12, 34

Baijan Daiquiri 130
Baijan Punch 52
Baijan Swizzle 96
Bali Fizz 72
balloon glasses 15
bananas 218
bar spoons 16
Baton Blanc 222
Bay Breeze 32
Bellini 62
Bénédictine 44, 176, 180

berries 26, 108, 220
Berry Collins 26
Betsy 188
bison grass vodka 72
bitter lemon 178
Bitter Spring 98
Bitter Sweet Sangria 70
Blanc Mont Blanc 170
blending 18
Blossom Tree Fizz 34
Blue Grass Punch 222
Blush Sangria 226
Boston glasses 15
Boston shakers 16
bottle openers 16
bourbon
Baton Blanc 222
Blue Grass Punch 222
Bourbon Mule 40
infused bourbon 12, 108
Mulled Orchard 216
Old-Fashioned 134
orange & cherry-infused bourbon 13, 40
Peach Smash 202
Rhett Butler 202
Southern Belle 216
Spiced Pear Punch 180
William's Pear 180
brandy 17
Abc Cocktail 154
apple brandy 50, 128
Brandy Alexander 148
cherry brandy 44
Classic Champagne Cocktail 90
ginger-infused cognac 12, 200
Jack Rose 128
Jaffa 148
La Rochelle Punch 220
Monte Carlo Sling 38
Moon River 168
Stone Jack Sour 128
Valencian Sangria 70
Brandy Alexander 148
Bucks Fizz 66

caçhaca 170
Camber Sands Iced Tea 82

Camomile Collins 42
Camomile Sangria 186
camomile tea 42, 88, 186
camomile & fennel seed shrub 11, 42
syrup 68
Campari
Baijan Daiquiri 130
Bitter Sweet Sangria 70
Gaseosa Tinto 228
Italian New Wave 112
Los Altos 48
Negroni 142
pineapple-infused Campari 13
Spagliagto 112
Torino Spritzer 228
Valencian Sangria 70
Caprissima da Framoesa 194
Caprissima da Uva 194
cardamom
Bali Fizz 72
ginger & green cardamom-infused gin 13
Zan La Cay 72
celery 190, 192
Chambord 58
Champagne
Bali Fizz 72
Classic Champagne Cocktail 90
French 75 68
Mandarin 75 92
Primrose Fizz 80
Riviera Fizz 90
Tanka Cobbler 92
Zan La Cay 72
Champagne glasses 14
Chartreuse 156
cherry brandy 44
Cherry Buck Mule 40
cherry-infused spirits 13
chocolate 148
cider 42, 216
cinnamon 166, 220
cinnamon-infused spirits 12
Citrus Highball 104
Classic Champagne

Cocktail 90
Classic Martini 140
clementines 104
Cloudy Cooler 186
Cobbled Summer 184
Cobbler Fizz 78
cocktail glasses 14
coconut cream 218
coffee liqueur 54
Cointreau
    the Fix 200
    Long Island Iced Tea 14, 82
    Maiden's Prayer 168
    Moon River 168
    Pancho Villa 118
    Singapore Sling 44
Colonial Punch 212
Copa Kaye 170
Cosmopolitan 150
Cotter Kir 76
coupette glasses 14
cranberry juice
    Bay Breeze 32
    Blue Grass Punch 222
    Blush Sangria 226
    Camber Sands Iced Tea 82
    Cosmopolitan 150
    Cotter Kir 76
    Playa del Mar 28
    Rhett Butler 202
    Sea Breeze 32
    Sex on the Beach 58
    Watermelon Martini 164
    Williamsburg 150
crème de banane 162
crème de cacao 148, 158, 162, 232
crème de cassis 76, 154
crème de framboise 76, 150, 154, 226
crème de menthe 162
crème de peche 72
Cuba Libre 14, 86
cucumber
    Bali Fizz 72
    Cucumber Rangoon 100
    cucumber-infused spirits 12, 100, 206
    Eden's Club Collins 30
    English Garden Fizz 234
    Gin Cucumber Cooler 30
    Gin Garden Martini 166
    Ichi Highball 24
    NonAlcoholic Jade's
        Cooler 190

Orchard Fizz 190
Paloma Verde 174
Pimm's Cocktail 230
Southside Royale 126
Zan La Cay 72

Daiquiri 130
double-straining 19
Drambuie 56
Duke's Daiquiri 196
Dusky Ricky 50
Dutch Rose 144

Earl Grey tea 82, 214
Eden's Club Collins 30
elderflower cordial
    Afternoon Watermelon 224
    Garden Cooler 234
    Gin Garden Martini 166
    Mocking Bird 114
    Non-Alcoholic Jade's
        Cooler 190
    Sakura Sangria 206
    White Sangria 206
elderflower liqueur 30, 80
English Garden Fizz 234

falernum 52, 96, 152, 194
fennel seed shrubs 11, 98, 220
Fino Highball 104
The Fix 200
flavoured syrups 9–11
food processors 16
French 75 68
French Afternoon 68
French Pink Lady 138
Fresh Paloma 174
fruit syrups 9–11

Galliano 160, 168, 218
Gaseosa Tinto 228
gin 17
    Berry Collins 26
    Betsy 188
    Camomile Collins 42
    Citrus Highball 104
    Cobbled Summer 184
    Earl's Punch 214
    Eden's Club Collins 30
    English Garden Fizz 234
    Fino Highball 104
    the Fix 200
    French 75 68
    French Afternoon 68

French Pink Lady 138
Garden Cooler 234
Gin Cucumber Cooler 30
Gin Garden Martini 166
Gin Sling 44
Ginger Langra 208
Ginny Gin Fizz 88
Ginty Collins 22
Green Bay Colada 182
infused gin 12, 13, 106
Kiwi Smash 182
Langra & Tonic 208
Long Island iced tea 14, 82
Maiden's Prayer 168
Martinez 144
Moon River 168
Negroni 142
Nehru 74
On the Lawn 230
Orange Blossom 200
Orchard Collins 42
Pimm's Cocktail 230
Poppin's Gin Fizz 120
Royal Cobbler 78
Singapore Sling 44
Smoky Martini 140
Soda Shop Collins 38
Southside 126
Southside Royale 126
Strawberry Fields 88
Sunshine State 80
Sylvestre Punch 214
Tom Collins 22
ginger 9, 84, 190
    infused spirits 12, 13, 208, 220
    Scotch Ginger Highball 46
ginger ale 46, 54, 220, 230
ginger beer 40, 52, 54
ginger juice
    Baijan Punch 52
    Cherry Buck Mule 40
    Cucumber Rangoon 100
    Green Bay Colada 182
    Highland Highball 46
    Highland Punch 56
    Penicillin 124
    Wrong Island Spiced Tea 84
Ginger Langra 208
ginger wine 56
Ginny Gin Fizz 88
Ginty Collins 22
glasses, choosing 14–15

Godmother 156
Golden Apricot 84
grapefruit/grapefruit juice
    Apple Jack Ricky 50
    Bitter Spring 98
    Caprissima da Framoesa 194
    Dusky Ricky 50
    Earl's Punch 214
    Fresh Paloma 174
    Ginty Collins 22
    Orange Blossom 200
    Paloma 48
    Paloma Verde 174
    Poppin's Gin Fizz 120
    Rising Sun 160
    St Marks Fizz 66
    Sakura Punch 226
    Sea Breeze 32
    Sylvestre Punch 214
    Tinto de Venezia 210
    Vespertilio 210
grapes 170, 186, 194
grappa 114
Grasshopper 19, 162
Green Bay Colada 182
grenadine 44, 74, 128, 144, 158, 196

Harvey Wallbanger 160
hawthorne strainers 16
hibiscus tea 120
highball glasses 14
Highland Highball 46
honey 56, 110
hurricane glasses 15

ice 8
Ichi highball 24
infused spirits 12–13
Iola's Punch 212
Italian New Wave 112

Jack Rose 128
Jade's Cooler 190
Jaffa 148
jiggers 16

Kir Royale 76
Kiwi Smash 182
kumquats 114

La Rochelle Punch 220
Langra & Tonic 208
layering 19

lemon grass vodka 26
lemon verbena tea 120
lemon vodka 82, 150, 178
lemonade 70, 230
lemons/lemon juice
  Afternoon Watermelon 224
  Annabella 146
  Apricot Collins 34
  Bali Fizz 72
  Baton Blanc 222
  Blanc Mont Blanc 170
  Blue Grass Punch 222
  Bourbon Mule 40
  Camber Sands Iced Tea 82
  Camomile Collins 42
  Camomile Sangria 186
  Cherry Buck Mule 40
  Cobbled Summer 184
  Colonial Punch 212
  Dusky Ricky 50
  English Garden Fizz 234
  Fino Highball 104
  French 75 68
  French Afternoon 68
  Gaseosa Tinto 228
  Gin Sling 44
  Ginger Langra 208
  Ginny Gin Fizz 88
  Green Bay Colada 182
  Highland Highball 46
  Highland Punch 56
  Jack Rose 128
  Kir Royale 76
  La Rochelle Punch 220
  Langra & Tonic 208
  lemon & ginger syrup 9
  Lemon Grass Collins 26
  Lola's Punch 212
  Long Island Iced Tea 14,
    82
  Mocking Bird 114
  Moon River 168
  Mulled Orchard 216
  Orchard Collins 42
  Peach Smash 202
  Penicillin 124
  Pisco Collins 114
  Riviera Fizz 90
  Royal Cobbler 78
  Rum Collins 96
  Sakura Sangria 206
  Scotch Ginger Highball 46
  Sherry Punch 184
  Soda Shop Collins 38
  Southern Belle 216

Spice Route Punch 220
Stone Jack Sour 128
Strawberry Fields 88
Sunshine State 80
Tom Collins 22
Torino Spritzer 228
Venetian Sling 98
Watermelon Punch 224
Watermelon Spritz 178
Whisky Sour 124
White Sangria 206
William's Pear 180
lime bitters 136
limes/lime juice
  Apple Martini 166
  Baijan Daiquiri 130
  Baijan Punch 52
  Baijan Swizzle 96
  Betsy 188
  Blush Sangria 226
  Caprissima da Framoesa
    194
  Caprissima da Uva 194
  Copa Kaye 170
  Cosmopolitan 150
  Cuba Libre 14, 86
  Daiquiri 130
  Duke's Daiquiri 196
  the Fix 200
  French Pink Lady 138
  Golden Apricot 84
  Limon Mojito 116
  Long Blush 110
  Los Altos 48
  Lucha Libre 86
  Margarita 138
  Melon Daiquiri 132
  Mexican Mule 54
  Mojito 116
  Moscow Mule 54
  Paloma 48
  Pisco Punch 152
  Pisco Sour 152
  Planter's Punch 232
  Playa del Mar 28
  Rhett Butler 202
  Rude Jude 198
  Rum Punch 218
  Sea Breeze 32
  Singapore Sling 44
  Southside 126
  Southside Royale 126
  Strawberry Daiquiri 132
  Summer Mary 36
  Tahitian mule 52

Tahitian Pearl 196
Tempo 232
Watermelon Martini 164
West Side Pink Flamingo
  188
Williamsburg 150
Wrong Island Spiced Tea
  84
Limon Mojito 116
Long Blush 110
Long Island Iced Tea 14, 82
Los Altos 48
Lucha Libre 86
Lychee Martini 146
lychees 146, 226

Maiden's Prayer 168
Mandarin 75 92
Mandarine Napoléon 148
mandarins 78
mangoes/mango juice
  Ambika Bellini 74
  Ginger Langra 208
  Langra & Tonic 208
  Lola's Punch 212
  mango-infused gin 13
  Mango Ricky 106
  Nehru 74
maple syrup 50
maraschino liqueur 154
Margarita 138
Margarita glasses 14
Martinez 144
Martini glasses 14
measures 16
Melon Daiquiri 132
Mexican Mule 54
Midori 132
mint
  Afternoon Watermelon 224
  Baijan Swizzle 96
  Camber Sands Iced Tea 82
  Eden's Club Collins 30
  English Garden Fizz 234
  Gin Cucumber Cooler 30
  Long Blush 110
  Mint Julep 108
  mint tea 106, 234
  mint-infused vodka 13
  Mojito 116
  Peach Smash 202
  Port Stinger 154
  Primrose Fizz 80
  Southside 126
  Southside Royale 126

Spiced Berry Julep 108
Strawberry Daiquiri 132
Sunshine State 80
Watermelon Smash 102
Watermelon Spritz 178
West Side Pink Flamingo
  188
mixing glasses 16
Mocking Bird 114
Mojito 18
Monte Carlo Sling 38
Moon River 168
Moscow Mule 54
muddling 18
muddling sticks 16
Mulled Orchard 216

Negroni 142
Nehru 74
Noilly Prat 118
nutmeg-infused spirits 12

Old-Fashioned 134
Old-Fashioned at Dusk 134
old-fashioned glasses 15
oleo-saccharum 10–11,
  46, 92
olives 118, 140
On the Lawn 230
orange bitters
  Dutch Rose 144
  Jaffa 148
  Lucha Libre 86
  Old-Fashioned 134
  Primera 142
  Rum Collins 96
  Smoky Martini 140
  Soda Shop Collins 38
  Stone Jack Sour 128
orange blossom water 34,
  144
orange liqueur 40, 52, 70,
  144
oranges/orange juice
  Apricot Collins 34
  Baton Blanc 222
  Bucks Fizz 66
  Dusky Ricky 50
  Harvey Wallbanger 160
  infused bourbon 13
  Maiden's Prayer 168
  Mandarin 75 92
  orange & fennel seed
    shrub 11, 98, 228
  Orange Blossom 200

Pisco Punch 152
Playa del Mar 28
Rum Punch 218
Sex on the Beach 58
Stone Jack Sour 128
Summer Mary 36
Sylvestre Punch 214
Tanka Cobbler 92
Tinto de Venezia 210
Valencian Sangria 70
Venetian Sling 98
Orchard Collins 42
Orchard Fizz 190

Paloma Verde 174
Pancho Villa 118
Parisian Fizz 64
passion fruit
　Copa Kaye 170
　juice 218
　liqueur 164
　Parisian Fizz 64
　Passion Fruit Spritz 110
　syrup 66, 104, 160, 186,
　　210
　Vespertilio 210
pastis 64, 138, 194
peach bitters 68, 80, 114
peach schnappes 58
peaches
　Bellini 62
　Duke's Daiquiri 196
　Garden Cooler 234
　juice 218
　Peach Smash 202
　Tahitian Pearl 196
pears 176, 180
peppercorns 36, 70, 74, 112
Peppermint Ricky 106
Pimm's No.1 100, 230
Pina Coco 218
pineapple/pineapple juice
　Baijan Daiquiri 130
　Baijan Punch 52
　Bay Breeze 32
　Cobbled Summer 184
　Colonial Punch 212
　the Fix 200
　infused spirits 13, 112
　Paloma Verde 174
　Pina Coco 218
　Pisco Punch 152
　Playa del Mar 28
　raspberry & pineapple
　　syrup 10, 78

Rum Punch 218
Sex on the Beach 58
Sex in the Dunes 58
Sherry Punch 184
Singapore Sling 44
Tahitian Pearl 196
Pink Cooler 178
Pink Sangria 120
pisco 114, 152
Playa del Mar 28
pomegranate juice 110, 120
port 154
pourers 16
Primera 142
Primrose Fizz 80
prosecco
　Ambika Bellini 74
　Bellini 62
　Bucks Fizz 66
　Cobbler Fizz 78
　French Afternoon 68
　Italian New Wave 112
　Kir Royale 76
　Nehru 74
　Parisian Fizz 64
　Rossini 64
　St Marks Fizz 66
　Southside Royale 126
　Spaqliaqto 112
　Sunshine State 80
　Vespertilio 210

raspberries
Berry Collins 26
Caprissima da Framoesa
　194
Cobbled Summer 184
Cobbler Fizz 78
Cotter Kir 76
French Pink Lady 138
Parisian Fizz 64
Poppin's Gin Fizz 120
Port Stinger 154
raspberry & pineapple
　syrup 10
Royal Cobbler 78
raspberry-infused Aperol
　13
Tanka Cobbler 92
Valentine Martini 164
raspberry liqueur 194
　crème de framboise 76,
　　150, 154, 226
raspberry syrup 184
raspberry vodka 164

Red Rum 198
red wine 70, 228
redcurrants 198
Rhett Butler 202
Rising Sun 160
Riviera Fizz 90
rocks glasses 15
rose syrup 9, 146, 226
rosé wine 76, 110, 120,
　188, 210, 226
Rossini 64
Royal Cobbler 78
Rude Jude 198
rum 17
　Baijan Daiquiri 130
　Baijan Punch 52
　Baijan Swizzle 96
　Caprissima da Framoesa
　　194
　Caprissima da Uva 194
　Colonial Punch 212
　Cuba Libre 14, 86
　Daiquiri 130
　Duke's Daiquiri 196
　Golden Apricot 84
　infused rum 12, 13, 52
　Limon Mojito 116
　Lola's Punch 212
　Long Island Iced Tea 14, 82
　Melon Daiquiri 132
　Mojito 116
　Pina Coco 218
　Planter's Punch 232
　Red Rum 198
　Rude Jude 198
　Rum Collins 96
　Rum Old-Fashioned 134
　Rum Punch 218
　Rum Rangoon 100
　Rum Refashioned 136
　Strawberry Daiquiri 132
　Tahitian mule 52
　Tempo 232
　Wrong Island Spiced Tea
　　84

St Marks Fizz 66
St Petersburg 156
Sakura Punch 226
Sakura Sangria 206
Scotch Ginger Highball 46
Sea Breeze 32
Sex on the Beach 58
Sex in the Dunes 58
shaking cocktails 18

sherry
　Cobbled Summer 184
　Cobbler Fizz 78
　Fino Highball 104
　Ginger Langra 208
　Royal Cobbler 78
　Sherry Punch 184
　Tanka Cobbler 92
shot glasses 15
shrubs 11
Silk Stocking 158
Singapore Sling 44
sloe gin 66, 90, 140, 198
Smoky Martini 140
Soda Shop Collins 38
Southern Belle 216
Southside 126
Southside Royale 126
Spice Route Punch 220
spice sugar syrup 10, 216
Spiced Berry Julep 108
Spiced Pear Punch 180
star anise-infused vodka
　13, 150
Stone Fence 176
Stone Jack Sour 128
Stone Stairs 176
strawberries
　Afternoon Watermelon 224
　Betsy 188
　Rossini 64
　Rude Jude 198
　Strawberry Daiquiri 132
　Strawberry Fields 88
　Strawberry Fizz 192
　Strawberry Smash
　　(non-alcoholic) 192
　West Side Pink Flamingo
　　188
strawberry syrup 26, 132,
　188, 198
Sylvestre Punch 214
syrup
　flavoured syrups 9–11
　sugar syrup 8–9

Tahitian Mule 52
Tahitian Pearl 196
tangerines 48
Tanka Cobbler 92
tea
　Camber Sands Iced Tea 82
　Camomile Sangria 186
　Citrus Highball 104
　Earl's Punch 214

English Garden Fizz 234
flavoured syrups 9
Garden Cooler 234
Ginty Collins 22
Peppermint Ricky 106
Pink Sangria 120
Poppin's Gin Fizz 120
Southern Belle 216
Strawberry Fields 88
Watermelon Smash 102
Wrong Island Spiced Tea 84
Tempo 232
tequila 17
Dirty Sanchez 118
Fresh Paloma 174
Long Island Iced Tea 14, 82
Los Altos 48
Lucha Libre 86
Margarita 138
Mexican Mule 54
Old-Fashioned at Dusk 134
Paloma 48
Pancho Villa 118
Playa del Mar 28
Primera 142
Silk Stocking 158
Sombrero 158
Tahitian Pearl 196
Tijuana Mary 36
Watermelon Smash 102
Tia Maria 118
Tijuana Mary 36
Tinto de Venezia 210
toddy glasses 15
Tom Collins 22
tomato juice 36
Torino Spritzer 228
Triple Sec
Cherry Buck Mule 40
Cosmopolitan 150

English Garden Fizz 234
French Pink Lady 138
Lucha Libre 86
Lychee Martini 146
Margarita 138
Stone Jack Sour 128
Torino Spritzer 228
Williamsburg 150

umeshu 24, 100, 206

Valencian Sangria 70
Valentine Martini 164
vanilla liqueur 26, 38
vanilla syrup 198
Venetian Sling 98
vermouth
Bitter Sweet Sangria 70
Blanc Mont Blanc 170
Classic Martini 140
Dutch Rose 144
Gaseosa Tinto 228
Italian New Wave 112
Martinez 144
Negroni 142
Primera 142
Spagliato 112
Torino Spritzer 228
Valencian Sangria 70
Vespertilio 210
vinegar 11
vodka 17
Afternoon Watermelon 224
Annabella 146
Apple Martini 166
Bali Fizz 72
Bay Breeze 32
Betsy 188
Blanc Mont Blanc 170
Blush Sangria 226
Camber Sands Iced Tea 82
Camomile Sangria 186

Cosmopolitan 150
Dutch Rose 144
Godmother 156
Harvey Wallbanger 160
infused vodka 12, 13, 34, 150, 206
Lemon Grass Collins 26
Long Blush 110
Long Island iced tea 14, 82
Lychee Martini 146
Moscow Mule 54
Peppermint Ricky 106
Pink Cooler 178
Rising Sun 160
St Petersburg 156
Sakura Punch 226
Sakura Sangria 206
Sea Breeze 32
Sex on the Beach 58
Sex in the Dunes 58
Summer Mary 36
Valentine Martini 164
Watermelon Martini 164
Watermelon Punch 224
West Side Pink Flamingo 188
White Sangria 206

watermelon
Afternoon Watermelon 224
Pink Cooler 178
Tijuana Mary 36
Watermelon Martini 164
Watermelon Punch 224
Watermelon Smash 102
Watermelon Spritz 178
West Side Pink Flamingo 188
West Side Pink Flamingo 188
whisky 17
Ginger Fix 56
Highland Highball 46

Highland Punch 56
Ichi highball 24
Old-Fashioned at Dusk 134
Penicillin 124
Scotch Ginger Highball 46
Stone Fence 176
Stone Stairs 176
Whisky Highball 24
Whisky Sour 124
White Sangria 206
white wine 98, 110, 186, 206, 212
Williamsburg 150
wine glasses 15
Wrong Island Spiced Tea 84

Zan La Cay 72

acknowledgements

Commissioning Editor: Eleanor Maxfield
Editor: Pauline Bache
Designer: Geoff Fennell
Special Photography: Jonathan Kennedy
Special Recipes and Styling: Tom Soden & Felix von Nida
Picture Library Manager: Jennifer Veall
Production Controller: Sarah Kramer

Special Photography © Octopus Publishing Group Limited/Jonathan Kennedy: Additional photography © Octopus Publishing Group Limited/Stephen Conroy